CAUGHT IN THE MIDDLE

Educational Reform for Young Adolescents in California Public Schools

**REPORT OF THE SUPERINTENDENT'S
MIDDLE GRADE TASK FORCE**

Publishing Information

Caught in the Middle: Educational Reform for Young Adolescents in California Public Schools was developed by State Superintendent Bill Honig's Middle Grade Task Force, which was cochaired by Gail G. Anderson and Robert L. Martin (see the Acknowledgments for a list of all the members of the task force). The principal writer of the document was James J. Fenwick. The report was designed by Fenwick Associates and was prepared for photo-offset production by Artifax Corporation, San Diego. The document, which was edited for publication by Theodore R. Smith, was published by the California Department of Education, 721 Capitol Mall, Sacramento, California (mailing address: P.O. Box 944272, Sacramento, CA 94244-2720); it was printed by the Office of State Printing, and it was distributed under the provisions of the Library Distribution Act and *Government Code* Section 11096.

ISBN 0-8011-0488-2

Ordering Information

Copies of this publication are available for $9.25 each, plus shipping and handling charges. California residents are charged sales tax. Orders may be sent to the Publications Division, Sales Office, California Department of Education, P.O. Box 271, Sacramento, CA 95812-0271; FAX (916) 323-0823. See page 162 for complete information on payment, including credit card purchases. Prices on all publications are subject to change.

A partial list of other educational resources available from the Department begins on page 161. In addition, an illustrated *Educational Resources Catalog* describing publications, videos, and other instructional media available from the Department can be obtained without charge by writing to the address given above or by calling the Sales Office at (916) 445-1260.

Contents

Appendix

Bibliography

Note:

There are twenty-two principles of middle grade education addressed in this report. Each principle is developed through a discussion which presents the logic of the Task Force. Included are illustrations, charts, diagrams, excerpts, and catalytic examples which amplify the text.

Each discussion concludes with specific recommendations which have implications for legislative initiatives, educational policies, administrative guidelines, and professional practices. The recommendations are directed to those who occupy leadership roles and who have the authority and power to give meaning and substance to the reform of middle grade education in California's public schools.

Middle grade students are unique. No other grade span encompasses such a wide range of intellectual, physical, psychological, and social development, and educators must be sensitive to the entire spectrum of these young people's capabilities. For many students the middle grades represent the last chance to develop a sense of academic purpose and personal commitment to educational goals. Those who fail at the middle grade level often drop out of school and may never again have the opportunity to develop to their fullest potential.

Caught in the Middle: Educational Reform for Young Adolescents in California Public Schools presents a reform agenda for grades six, seven, and eight—the middle grades. The report culminates one year of research and public hearings conducted by the Middle Grade Task Force to learn what makes effective schooling at the middle grade level. This report is intended to stimulate open discussion and debate. For too long, the middle grades have been treated as a wild card for solving facilities and enrollment problems. Now it is time to face the critical educational issues at stake in these "neglected grades."

The success of the educational reform movement depends on meeting the needs of middle grade students—both academically and socially. Failing to address these needs jeopardizes efforts for educational excellence and, more importantly, for these students' own future success.

The most effective instruction at the middle grade level emphasizes academic integrity while making an emotional connection with students. Teachers and principals neither sacrifice academic excellence, nor expect their students to go from classroom to classroom without offering them support. The schools have a special spirit. They prove that academics and the emotional connection are not inconsistent. Students feel that they are part of a family.

Choices which affect the futures of students take shape in the self-contained classrooms of the early elementary years—a world organized by the teacher. For many students, it is a time of undefeated hopes and dreams of the future.

By the time these students enter high school, they have traveled a long way—both emotionally and academically. They now encounter a world of hallways, lockers, cafeterias, and a multitude of classrooms. They will be sustained by peers and daydreams, as much as by teachers and course content. The all-purpose teacher of their childhood has been replaced by a printed schedule, departmentalized classrooms, and one five-hundredth of a counselor. Some students will thrive in this environment; many others will become defeated.

Between the worlds of the elementary and secondary schools are the middle grades. In these grades, the hopes we have for all students are tested from two directions—by the students' own maturation and by the demands made on them for academic preparation. The first challenge for schools which enroll middle grade students is to make sure that they are "connected" to the goals and purposes of their schools in positive ways and have an opportunity to increase their self-esteem. Young adolescents become intensively self-conscious and self-evaluative. Middle grade schools must provide students with a caring transition as they move from elementary to high school. The second challenge is to prepare students for academic success in high school. The aspirations reflected in this report are for all students—whether they are in regular, special, bilingual, or compensatory education classes.

Reconciling these two primary challenges—the personal and the academic—with the developmental characteristics of young adolescents represents the unifying theme of this report. Young adolescents are intensely curious about the very questions which should be at the center of the language arts/social studies curricula. These subjects address many of the same questions that students ask themselves. Who am I? What do I want to be ? What is important? Schools which avoid these questions in the curriculum are missing a great opportunity to capture the imagination of students and to provide a curriculum emphasis common to all students, regardless of skill levels.

Perhaps the most critical aspect of these transitional years for students is the change from one teacher to many teachers. The faculty and the schedule must be organized so that small groups of teachers share the same students and are enabled to work together collegially. The investment in collegial faculty relationships is the hallmark of the most successful middle schools. This kind of rapport leads to shared planning and creative improvements in curriculum and instruction. It is also the basis for providing sound advice to students. Professional counseling services gain in effectiveness when supported by broad based faculty involvement in advisory programs.

I urge you to study this report. How do your schools compare? What is happening to your middle grade students? The middle grades are a critical time in these students' schooling. Each school board, superintendent, principal, counselor, and teacher shares in the responsibility to bring about middle grade educational reform across our state.

This report presents the findings and recommendations of the Middle Grade Task Force commissioned by Bill Honig, California Superintendent of Public Instruction. The uniqueness of middle grade education is emphasized. The case is made for the urgency of major educational reform in grades 6, 7, and 8. The concept of academic integrity is heavily emphasized as is the need for attention to the personal and social development of young adolescents. The tension between these issues is squarely faced. They are shown to be directly related and complementary to each other in contrast to being the basis for bitter and divisive professional arguments about relative educational priorities.

Middle grade students must experience the meaning of high standards of academic excellence in a school setting which recognizes the importance of personal "connectedness." This concept conveys a special sense of belonging, of being accepted by teachers and peers. The personal connection is critical for students of all ages. It is of special significance in early adolescence because it is in the middle grades that lifelong values begin to be shaped, including those that relate to academic achievement and personal commitment to educational goals.

The urgency of middle grade educational reform is accentuated by the gravity of dropout statistics. Nationwide data indicate that 700,000 students drop out of school annually. Unless dramatic changes occur which capture the intellects and emotions of young adolescents, this loss of human potential will continue to intensify. At present, the middle grades represent the last substantive educational experience for hundreds of thousands of students. If students fail to achieve the integration of their personalities and the motivation required to make a commitment to academic values by the end of the middle grades, many will never do so.

For all middle grade students there is a compelling need to ensure an intellectually stimulating school environment. This concept is repeatedly emphasized throughout this report. Special stress is given to the unfolding intellectual power of the minds of young adolescents and the critical need for new instructional strategies and organizational models which have the capacity to translate the principles of middle grade educational reform into the real world of students and teachers.

Gail G. Anderson   Robert L. Martin
Co-chairpersons
Middle Grade Task Force

ACKNOWLEDGMENTS

Middle Grade Task Force Members

Gail G. Anderson
Co-Chairperson
Superintendent
Orinda Union Elementary School District

Robert L. Martin
Co-Chairperson
Assistant Superintendent, Region C
Los Angeles Unified School District

Bonnie Bethel, Counselor
Washington Middle School
Vista Unified School District

Harriet Borson, Education Commission
California Congress of Parents,
Teachers, and Students, Inc.
Beverly Hills

Andre Brooks, Student Representative
Berkeley Unified School District

Maria Casillas-McGrath, Administrator
Los Angeles Unified School District

Yvette del Prado, Superintendent
Cupertino Union Elementary School
District

William Ellerbee, Jr., Principal
Jedediah Smith Elementary School
Sacramento City Unified School District

Carolina L. Erie, Director of Curriculum
Conejo Valley Unified School District

James J. Fenwick, Executive Director
Fenwick Associates, San Diego

Arturo M. Flores, Director
Professional Development/
Bilingual Education
Hanford Elementary School District

Jane Gawronski
Assistant Superintendent
Walnut Valley Unified School District

Jackie Goldberg, Member
Board of Education
Los Angeles Unified School District

Lucille Gonzales, Director
State and Federal Programs
Pomona Unified School District

Jennie Spencer Green, Professor
The California State Polytechnic
University, Pomona

Alfred Guenther, Teacher
Stephen M. White Junior High School
Los Angeles Unified School District

Jo Gusman, Teacher
Ethel Phillips Elementary School
Sacramento City Unified School District

Hal Hendrickson, President
Board of Education
Morgan Hill Unified School District

Mary Humphrey
Teacher Representative
California Teachers Association
Buena Park Elementary School District

Duncan Johnson, Superintendent
Fullerton Elementary School District

Janet Kierstead, Consultant
Research and Curriculum Development
Westlake Village

Evaline Khayat Kruse, Teacher
Audubon Junior High School
Los Angeles Unified School District

John R. Mergendoller
Senior Program Director
Far West Laboratory, San Francisco

Charles Palmer, Principal
Bret Harte Preparatory
Intermediate School
Los Angeles Unified School District

Paula Katz Pitluk, Representative
California Federation of Teachers
Librarian and Mentor Teacher
ABC Unified School District

Corazon A. Ponce
Program Administrator
Bilingual Education Department
San Francisco Unified School District

Sally Rayhill, Representative
Association of California School
Administrators
Principal, Harvest Park
Intermediate School, Pleasanton Joint
Elementary School District

Myra Redick, Assistant Superintendent
Mt. Diablo Unified School District

Annie Richardson, Parent Education
Los Angeles Unified School District

Joseph Rost
Professor of Education
University of San Diego

Becky Sargent, Member
Board of Education
Redondo Beach City
Elementary School District

Dorothy Smith, Member
Board of Education
San Diego City Unified School District

Neil Snyder, Principal
Conejo Elementary School
Conejo Valley Unified School District

Bruce F. Thompson, President
California League of Middle Schools
Superintendent
Woodside Elementary School District

David Winters, Teacher
Santa Barbara Junior High School
Santa Barbara High School District

James G. Zoll, Principal
Coronado Middle School
Coronado Unified School District

Task Force Staff

Phil Daro
Assistant Superintendent
Office of Project Development
California State Department of
Education

Vicky Campbell
Analyst
Office of Project Development
California State Department of
Education

James J. Fenwick
Principal Writer
Fenwick Associates
San Diego

ACKNOWLEDGMENTS

Regional Panel Members

Region I

Joseph Appel
Shasta Union High School District

Marla Benoit
Elk Grove Unified School District

Kathleen Bond
Fairfield-Suisun Unified School District

Candy Carter
Tahoe-Truckee Unified School District

Joan Culver
San Juan Unified School District

Linda Ferrick
San Juan Unified School District

Lois L. Graham
Sacramento City Unified School District

George Hayden
Sacramento City Unified School District

Dan Kenley
Lincoln Unified School District

David Klasson
Whitmore Union Elementary School District

Bart Lagomarsino
Elk Grove Unified School District

Fred Pasquini
Sacramento City Unified School District

Shirley Patch
San Juan Unified School District

Ishmael Rasul
Sacramento City Unified School District

Doug Usedom
Yuba City Unified School District

Virginia Woods
Sacramento City Unified School District

Region II

Laurelynn Brooks
Bakersfield Elementary School District

Diane Caspary
Merced City Elementary School District

Bob Hill
Fresno Unified School District

Jim Holmes
Fresno Unified School District

David McCauley
Fresno Unified School District

Jeanette Phillips
Fresno Unified School District

Pam Scortt
Central Unified School District

Region III

Susan Adams
Milpitas Unified School District

Joy Addison
Palo Alto Unified School District

Sharon Belshaw
Fremont Unified School District

Yetive Bradley
Oakland Unified School District

John Brand
Redwood City Elementary School District

Thomas Bye
Vallejo City Unified School District

Jim Fletcher
Modesto City High School District

Charles A. Foster, Jr.
Foundation for Teaching Economics, San Francisco

Lea Frey
Los Gatos Union Elementary School District

Sharon Fritz
Millbrae Elementary School District

Andrew Garrido
Cupertino Union Elementary School District

Rudy Gatti
Santa Clara Unified School District

Joanne Grim
Oakland Unified School District

Mae Johnson
Monterey Peninsula Unified School District

Susan Kovalic
San Jose

Pat Lamson
Cupertino Union Elementary School District

Robert J. McCarthy
San Leandro Unified School District

Sharon McQueen
San Carlos Elementary School District

Marilyn Miller
San Jose Unified School District

Linda Page
Fremont

Roger Tom
San Francisco Unified School District

Louis Towner
San Jose Unified School District

Gene Unger
Santa Clara Unified School District

Arturo Vasquez
Healdsburg Union High School District

Robert Welch
Burlingame Elementary School District

Adam Wolf
Cotati-Rohnert Park Unified School District

Louise Zick
Santa Clara Unified School District

Region IV

Rudy Aguilera
Santa Barbara High School District

Dick Jamgochian
University of California, Santa Barbara

Robert Keatinge
Carpinteria Unified School District

John Prince
Simi Valley Unified School
District

Andrew Smidt
Ojai Unified School District

Tim Stenson
Santa Barbara Elementary
School District

William Tracy
Santa Barbara

Region V ("A" and "B")

Minerva Gandara Boggs
El Rancho Unified School
District

Robert W. Bruesch
Rosemead Elementary School
District

Sharon Cook
Bonita Unified School District

Leonard Duff
Pomona Unified School District

Norman Eisen
Whittier Union High School
District

Helen Fried
ABC Unified School District

Cassandra George
Pomona Unified School District

Renee E. Jackson
Los Angeles Unified School
District

Laurel Kanthak
Walnut Valley Unified School
District

Marilyn Landau
Los Angeles Unified School
District

Elane Polin
Redondo Beach City Elementary
School District

Mary Purucker
Los Angeles Unified School
District

Sharon Robison
Rowland Unified School District

Al Schifini
Los Angeles County
Superintendent of Schools Office

Estelle L. Schultz
Compton Unified School District

Chuck Smith
Moorpark Unified School
District

Billie Telles
Los Angeles County
Superintendent of Schools Office

Marilyn Zimmer
Glendale Unified School District

Barbara Zussman
Beverly Hills Unified School
District

Region VI

Jo Ann Ball
Placentia Unified School District

Ronald Berry
Buena Park Elementary School
District

Mark Campaigne
The Bishop's School, La Jolla

Janice Cook
La Mesa-Spring Valley
Elementary School District

Sherland Dirksen
La Mesa-Spring Valley
Elementary School District

Bob Erikson
Saddleback Valley Unified
School District

Joe Fazio
Cardiff Elementary School
District

Mike Foster
Vista Unified School District

Douglas E. Giles
Santee Elementary School
District

Katie E. "Betsy" Gilhland
San Diego City Unified School
District

Vicky Gorham
Vista Unified School District

Charmon Lehew
La Mesa-Spring Elementary
Valley School District

Judie Lowman
Fountain Valley Elementary
School District

Gary Mantee
La Habra City Elementary School
District

James Mason, Educational
Consultant
Anaheim

Peter McHugh
Vista Unified School District

Bruce Murphy
Santee Elementary School
District

Jesse Perry
San Diego City Unified School
District

Robert Purvis
Buena Park Elementary School
District

James Raymond
Cajon Valley Union Elementary
School District

Mary C. Sable
La Mesa-Spring Valley
Elementary School District

Robert Simpson
Saddleback Valley Unified
School District

Isabella Skidmore
San Diego City Unified School
District

Lawrence S. Sykoff
La Jolla Country Day School

Joseph Tafoya
San Diego City Unified School
District

Steve Tarkington
Vista Unified School District

Aileen Teague
La Mesa-Spring Valley
Elementary School District

John D. Tennant
Irvine Unified School District

Ron Trotter
La Mesa-Spring Valley
Elementary School District

Kenneth Tye, Professor
Chapman College

Marilyn Wilkinson
La Mesa-Spring Valley
Elementary School District

Linda Wisher
Moreno Valley Unified School
District

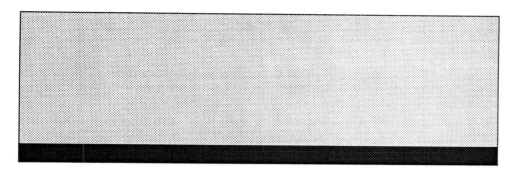

PART ONE

CURRICULUM AND INSTRUCTION:

Achieving Academic Excellence

1 Core Curriculum

Every middle grade student should pursue a common, comprehensive, academically oriented core curriculum irrespective of primary language or ethnic background.

Educated persons possess an informed perspective about themselves and their society. This perspective is developed through knowledge, skills, and ideals which provide the foundation for reasoned decisions about personal, civic, and economic rights and responsibilities.

The concept of a common, comprehensive, academically oriented core curriculum evolves directly from this definition. It is the basis of a brave commitment to the goal of a fully educated citizenry. There is no nation in the world more seriously attempting to attain this goal than ours. There is no state more ready than California to provide new national leadership in this effort. There is no more critical period than the middle grades to pursue this goal.

A common core of knowledge exists which all educated citizens should possess. This core includes lessons to be gained from the study of literature, history, science, mathematics, and the arts. These lessons should be the legacy of every middle grade student. This point deserves the strongest possible emphasis. Vast numbers of California's middle grade population continue to need the intense support provided through ESL (English as a second language) and bilingual education programs in order to gain access to the full range of intellectual development represented by the core curriculum.

There is a common core of knowledge that all educated citizens should possess. By opening vistas for students into the broad achievements and issues of civilization, this core will empower students to participate in and benefit from a higher quality life. This core includes cultural literacy, scientific literacy, knowledge of the humanities, and appreciation of the values that undergird our society. In addition, through this core curriculum, students should develop fully the skills of reading, writing, speaking, listening, calculating, and learning and the ability to think critically. All students should have access to the core curriculum. Most students are expected to succeed in this rigorous academic curriculum.[1]

The content of core curriculum subjects must be linked to the heightened curiosity of young adolescents about themselves – who

1 *Secondary School Program Quality Criteria.* Prepared under the direction of the Office of School Improvement. Sacramento: California State Department of Education, ©1985, p. vii.

A Shared Heritage

Most school teachers, college professors, journalists, and social commentators agree that the general background knowledge of American students is too low and getting lower. Surveys document great gaps in students' basic knowledge of geography, history, literature, politics, and democratic principles. Teaching is hindered if teachers cannot count on their students sharing a body of knowledge, references, and symbols.

Every society maintains formal and informal mechanisms to transmit understanding of its history, literature, and political institutions from one generation to the next. A shared knowledge of these elements of our past helps foster social cohesion and a sense of national community and pride.

In the United States, the national community comprises diverse groups and traditions; together these have created a rich cultural heritage. Cultural literacy not only enables students to read better and gain new knowledge; it enables them to understand the shared heritage, institutions, and values that draw Americans together.

What Works: Research About Teaching and Learning. Prepared under the direction of William J. Bennett. Washington, D.C.: United States Department of Education, 1986, p. 53.

they are, how they fit into the world around them, how that world functions, and what exciting prospects for their lives lie beyond the immediate horizons of their present knowledge and experience.

Educators must help middle grade students wrestle with answers to these questions. Young adolescents must learn to draw upon the vast reservoir of accumulated knowledge available to them and to see its meaning for the dynamic, rapidly changing world which they are about to inherit. Unless this connection occurs in the middle grades, students risk trivial, superficial responses to the personal challenges which they will encounter throughout their lives.

The core curriculum for the middle grades needs much clearer definition than it has had for the past two decades. This definition has begun with both a professional and public consensus embodied in the *Model Curriculum Guides: K–8* and the new curriculum frameworks developed by the California State Department of Education. These documents articulate with the *Model Curriculum Standards* adopted in 1984 for grades 9–12.

Beyond this statewide definition, further degrees of specificity are needed at district, school, and classroom levels in order to respond to the complexity and diversity of over one thousand California school districts ranging in size from a single classroom to those with enrollments of more than one-half million students.

In order to achieve the level of

A Joyful Art

Dressed as Michelangelo, with paint smears on a flowing tunic, Frank Smith gave a speech recently to Massachusetts superintendents and school committee members. Only, he read to them from Euripides, Sophocles, Sappho and Dante to the music of a Gregorian chant. This Wayland ... teacher took them to "the world of low tech," to the joyful art of teaching.

"There is excitement in the world of my discipline; it is ever expanding, ever challenging both to the student and myself. The classical and medieval worlds are populated by men and women of genius. To introduce my students to this world is the most rare of all pleasures. It is a gift not offered to any but the teacher....

"Perhaps you want to know what the secret is that each teacher has in his or her soul. Every morning that I get up and start off to school, I'm excited about several things. One, I'm going to be dealing with young people. Two, I have a great secret that none of you share, unless you are a teacher ... When I go into the classroom and we gather together as a class, we call upon Virgil and Horace and Catullus and Michelangelo and all the great men and women of literature and the arts and music and science. We ask them to join with us. We listen to them, we ask them questions, and we learn from them. That is the secret."

Education USA, Vol. 28 (April 7, 1986), p. 249, ©1986. Reprinted by permission from *Education USA*, National School Public Relations Association.

clarity required for the middle grade core curriculum, students in grades 6, 7, and 8 should study a full, balanced repertoire of subjects which include:

- Reading/Literature
- Language Arts
- Mathematics
- Science (including Health)
- History and Geography
- Visual and Performing Arts
- Physical Education (including Health)
- Advisory (Group Guidance)
- Elective/Exploratory Courses

In addition, the opportunity to acquire proficiency in a second language is strongly encouraged for all middle grade students through elective/exploratory curricula. Students must be prepared to participate in the global economy of the 21st century. The study of English, Spanish, Japanese, Chinese, and Russian are particularly encouraged as languages representative of vast segments of the world's population.

The core curriculum is designed to provide students with a broad academic foundation needed for success in high school. It is also intended to extend their ability substantially to exercise postsecondary options related to academic and employment opportunities. These options have the potential to enrich individual lives and to strengthen the fabric of the larger society.

TASK FORCE RECOMMENDATIONS

❶ Local school boards should define middle grade curriculum policies which include the following provisions.

Recommended policy:

a. Students in grades 6, 7, and 8 shall pursue a common, comprehensive, academically oriented core curriculum which prepares them for success in high school and which provides them with the foundation required to exercise future academic and career options. This curriculum shall be appropriate to the developmental characteristics of young adolescents. Students shall experience instructional balance among

Continued on next page

RECOMMENDATIONS *Continued*

subjects in keeping with the following provisions:

Subjects	Average Minutes Per Week[1]
Reading/Literature	250
Language Arts[2]	250
Mathematics	250
Science (and Health)[3]	250
History and Geography	250
Visual and Performing Arts	125
Physical Education (and Health)[3]	200
Advisory (Group Guidance)	50
Elective/Exploratory Courses[4]	175
Total	**1,800**

1 The average number of minutes per week represents an average derived from the total of the three middle grade years. The average number of minutes per week for a given subject may differ at varying points during the three-year period.

2 Language Arts curricula emphasize direct instruction in writing, speaking, and vocabulary development.

3 Portions of the Health curriculum are covered in both Science and Physical Education curricula.

4 The opportunity to acquire proficiency in a second language is strongly encouraged for all middle grade students within the options provided through elective/exploratory courses.

The curricula in each subject shall be comparable to the standards established in the *Model Curriculum Guides: K–8* adopted by the California State Department of Education.

Continued on next page

RECOMMENDATIONS *Continued*

> **Note:** Suggestions for scheduling these subjects are provided in the chapter entitled "Scheduling: An Expression of Middle Grade Philosophy" found elsewhere in this report. These suggestions are based on 360 minutes of instructional time per day. Many districts will have more or less instructional time. Regardless of the length of the school day, none of these subjects should be omitted from any student's program. Schools on shorter instructional schedules should use a combination of flexible scheduling strategies and an integration of two or more subjects in order to include the recommended curricula.

b. Allocations of resources required to implement the middle grade curriculum shall be reviewed regularly by the district administration in consultation with the professional staff of each school; recommendations shall be submitted annually to the school board by the superintendent for purposes of allocating or reallocating resources required to maintain and/or improve the quality of curriculum and instructional practices in the middle grades consistent with district policies.

c. *Elective* curricula *may* require predefined levels of knowledge and skills mastery.

d. *Exploratory* curricula shall enable students to enroll in courses without predefined levels of knowledge and skills mastery.

e. The development of study skills shall be emphasized throughout all courses in the core, elective, and exploratory curricula.

Continued on next page

RECOMMENDATIONS *Continued*

f. **Performance expectations for freshmen entering high school shall be adopted for each subject in the core curriculum. These expectations shall exceed proficiency levels. They shall be defined in terms of applications of knowledge and skills to assigned projects which students are able to complete.**

Performance expectations shall be stated clearly and formally communicated to students and parents at regularly scheduled intervals.

Performance expectations shall relate to requirements needed to pursue the widest possible range of academic options (curriculum paths) in high school.

> **Note: Statements of performance expectations shall be consistent with other recommendations contained in this report. Examples of project criteria capable of satisfying performance expectations include the ability to:**
> - **Select a contemporary issue of special interest.**
> - **Relate this issue to historical events.**
> - **Conduct informal opinion surveys.**
> - **Prepare a written report which relates the selected issue to past events and current opinions.**
> - **Draw conclusions and/or formulate hypotheses.**
> - **Present an oral report to peers (or other appropriate audience), using visual and written materials.**

2 Knowledge

Every middle grade student should be empowered with the knowledge derived from studying the ideas, experiences, and traditions found in the core, elective, and exploratory curricula.

1 "All Children Need the Power of Knowledge, Ravitch Says," *ASCD Update*, Vol. 28 (May, 1986), p. 3. Reprinted with permission of the Association for Supervision and Curriculum Development. ©1986 by the Association for Supervision and Curriculum Development. All rights reserved.

Young adolescents have a natural curiosity about the world in which they live. They must have multiple exciting opportunities to explore this world through exposure to ideas, experiences, and traditions. Their instructional materials and classroom experiences should expose them to many of the enduring literary classics – especially those which have themes capable of exciting and challenging youthful imaginations. Their study of history, geography, science, mathematics, and the arts should allow them to discover the contributions of famous individuals of varied ethnic and linguistic backgrounds who have helped to give our society its rich cultural heritage.

Too often, this is not the case. Diane Ravitch comments about this contradiction:

Progress toward literary fluency is discouraged in elementary school by vapid, stilted, and fragmented readers. They are now used as late as the 8th grade ... and they preempt time to read enduring classics, which in their universality help children find meaning in their lives.

Repelled by the vacuous banality of school subjects, children look for heroes and romance in the trifles of popular culture. Exit Noah's Ark. Enter Love Boat. And not far behind trail large numbers of people who are culturally bereft and are thus likely to be passive recipients of a culture shaped by others.[1]

Students require access to a broad background of knowledge about their world. All written and spoken language is steeped in references to "ideas, experiences, and traditions" which help to shape their thoughts and mold their values.

The less students know about the background to which authors and speakers make reference, the less they are capable of relating to their world. The less they share in

Cultural Literacy

Part of our skill in reading and in writing is skill not just with linguistic structures but with words. Words are not purely formal counters of language; they represent large underlying domains of content. Part of language skill is content skill. As Apeneck Sweeney profoundly observed: "I gotta use words when I talk to you."...

Every writer is aware that the subtlety and complexity of what can be conveyed in writing depends on the amount of relevant tacit knowledge that can be assumed in readers. As psycholinguists have shown, the explicitly stated words on the page often represent the smaller part of the literary transaction. Some of this assumed knowledge involves such matters as generic conventions, that is, what to expect in a business letter, a technical report, a detective story, etc. An equally significant part of the assumed knowledge – often a more significant part – concerns tacit knowledge of the experiential realities embraced by the discourse. Not only have I gotta use words to talk to you, I gotta assume you know *something* about what I am saying. If I had to start from scratch, I couldn't start at all.

... Even a writer for an astrophysics journal must assume a "common reader" for the subculture being addressed. A newspaper writer must also assume a "common reader" but for a much bigger part of the culture, perhaps for the literate culture as a whole. In our own culture, Jefferson wanted to create a highly informed "common reader," and he must have assumed the real existence of such a personage when he said he would prefer newspapers without government to government without newspapers. But, without appropriate, tacitly shared background knowledge, people cannot understand newspapers. A certain extent of shared, canonical knowledge is inherently necessary to a literate democracy.

Continued on next page

the knowledge of the beauty, complexity, diversity, and mystery of their existence, the more constricted and impotent they become in their ability to communicate with others.

Students who are deprived of access to the broad background of knowledge shared widely within their society will experience great difficulty in understanding direct and implied meanings of generalizations, concepts, and ideas that could have empowered them to have a say in both their own and their society's future. Acquisition of this fund of widely shared general knowledge is termed "cultural literacy."

Research evidence has been accumulating in recent years which strongly suggests that beyond the second or third grade, the major factor determining reading proficiency is general background knowledge. The problem is complex and circular. Reading proficiency is diminished by lack of background knowledge, which, in turn, results in the inability of students to continue to gain the very knowledge which could enhance their reading skills.

The problem is further complicated by the fact that textbooks and related curriculum materials often discourage students and teachers alike. The verdict of the Carnegie Corporation echoes the observations of Ravitch cited earlier:

Many students' failure to perform close to their potential starts in upper elementary school, where the material is often so boring...that student interest and self-confidence wanes.[2]

> Continued from previous page
>
> For this canonical information I have proposed the term "cultural literacy." It is the translinguistic knowledge on which linguistic literacy depends. You cannot have the one without the other.
>
> ... School materials contain unfamiliar materials that promote the "acculturation" that is a universal part of growing up in any tribe or nation. Acculturation into a national literate culture might be defined as learning what the "common reader" of a newspaper in a literate culture could be expected to know. That would include knowledge of certain values (whether or not one accepted them), and knowledge of such things as (for example) the First Amendment, Grant and Lee, and DNA. In our own culture, what should these contents be? Surely our answer to that should partly define our school curriculum. Acculturation into a literate culture (the minimal aim of schooling; we should aim still higher) could be defined as the gaining of cultural literacy.
>
> E. D. Hirsch, Jr., "Cultural Literacy," Reprinted from *The American Scholar*, Volume 52, Number 2 (Spring, 1983), pp. 164-66. ©1983 by the author. By permission of the publisher.

There must be a vast improvement in the quality and availability of middle grade instructional materials if the goal of cultural literacy is to be achieved. A vital core curriculum must be facilitated by rich, diverse instructional materials. The sources of knowledge available to middle grade students must be of high quality, attractive, and compelling in their power to capture and hold the attention and imaginations of young adolescents.

Middle grade students need opportunities to explore the wide range of academic interests which are beginning to attract them. Their emerging capacity for abstract thought allows them to have insight into the magnitude of knowledge existing beyond their immediate experiences.

Paralleling the core curriculum are two essential types of curricula which should be available in the

better textbooks → goal of cultural literacy

> more $?
> how else ?

2 *A Nation Prepared: Teachers for the 21st Century.* Washington, D.C.: Carnegie Forum on Education and the Economy, ©1986, p. 75. This report was prepared by the Carnegie Forum on Education and the Economy's Task Force on Teaching as a Profession. The Carnegie Forum is a program of the Carnegie Corporation of New York.

middle grades. The first type encourages students to pursue individual interests. Pursuit of these interests should be woven into core academic subjects, elective courses, and extracurricular and intramural programs.

The second kind of curriculum is exploratory in nature. It allows students to survey broad themes and topics of potential interest to them. These studies can open doors to new categories of knowledge and skills and can give students a broadened sense of the scope of academic, vocational, and avocational possibilities available to them as adults.

There are multiple ways to make room for elective and exploratory curricula in the school program. These may include learning experiences scheduled within or without the regular school day.

The ACT-SO program (Afro-Academic, Cultural, Technological, Science Olympics), for example, uses hundreds of volunteers to teach Saturday enrichment classes. Every community has individuals with special abilities willing to share their knowledge and skill in similar ways. Many have never been approached to do so.

However implemented, elective and exploratory curricula are for all students in the middle grades. No student should be deprived of the intellectual stimulation found in pursuing areas of special interest or in exploring new categories of information and knowledge. Neither basic skills mastery nor English language proficiency should be required as conditions for enrolling in elective or exploratory courses.

A vital factor affecting the personal future of all students is their relative ability to pursue more advanced studies successfully in high school – and beyond high school. Courses found in the middle grade core, elective, and exploratory curricula have both intrinsic and extrinsic value. In the latter sense, they provide the stepping stones to further academic and vocational pursuits. The knowledge and skills essential for success in secondary and postsecondary curricula should receive priority attention in all middle grade courses. This goal should be seen as both parallel and complementary to efforts which encour-

ACT-SO

Hundreds of volunteers teach Saturday enrichment classes to young black students in 350 cities across the nation, including major urban areas throughout California.

The program is called ACT-SO (Afro-Academic, Cultural, Technological, Science Olympics). It doesn't cost the government a penny. One paid employee runs the program.

Students compete in 21 different categories, including creative writing, dramatics, music, computer science, biology, and many others. Winners compete nationally during the annual convention of the NAACP (National Association for the Advancement of Colored People).

Corporate sponsors pay for the gold, silver and bronze medals, the cash awards, and the travel expenses of the 450 local finalists who compete nationally. Ninety California corporations are among the contributors.

ACT-SO represents a major creative effort to enable students to explore and discover new areas of knowledge and information. The message is loud and clear. It is captured in the ACT-SO theme "Black is Brilliant." The model is powerful. It is adaptable in multiple ways ranging from a single school to an entire district. Size and scope are not the issue, nor is race. The ultimate value lies in helping all students enjoy and respect their expanding curiosity and to experience the intrinsic rewards which come with the increased intellectual power of young adolescence.

age students to explore personal interests and new categories of knowledge and skills as they experience and enjoy their expanding intellectual curiosity.

TASK FORCE RECOMMENDATIONS

❶ **Local school boards should define middle grade curriculum policies which include the following provisions.**

Recommended policy:

Every student's study of the core and exploratory curricula shall give priority to learning what is most appropriate and critical to the academic needs and intellectual interests of young adolescents.

These needs and interests include:

a. **A study of literary and historical works needed to understand generalizations and concepts which are basic to cultural literacy; this knowledge shall be gained through the study of ideas, experiences, and traditions which engage the natural curiosity of young adolescents and shall enable students:**

   (1) **To reflect on who they are as individuals, how their world functions, and how they fit into that world**

   (2) **To develop new levels of reading proficiency through an expanded comprehension of metaphors, similes, allegories, and other types of references and comparisons commonly used by authors in developing concepts and generalizations**

Continued on next page

RECOMMENDATIONS *Continued*

(3) **To relate successfully to the larger society and to become responsible, self-sufficient citizens**

(4) **To gain an expanded sense of the scope of the academic, vocational, and avocational opportunities open to them as adults**

b. **The knowledge and skills in each subject which are central to preparation for and successful completion of required high school curricula**

❷ **Teachers and principals should adapt or invent scheduling arrangements which facilitate the participation of every student in elective and exploratory curricula without compromising instruction in the core curriculum or conflicting with the provision of student support services.**

❸ **Superintendents and principals should draw on the availability of varied community resources to enable or enhance the provision of a wide range of elective and exploratory curricula for the middle grades.**

3 Thinking and Communication

Every middle grade student should develop the capacities for critical thought and effective communication.

Students in the middle grades experience a rapid unfolding of their intellectual capacities. There is a dramatic emergence of the ability to think reflectively – to think about thinking. This ability opens the way for more complex and abstract thought processes. These have profound implications for the development of moral reasoning, problem solving, critical thinking, and the ability to use scientific methods and make aesthetic judgments.

These capacities must be matched educationally by curricula and instructional practices which demand both thought and thoughtful communication in the classroom. Students can and must learn to think and to communicate effectively. They should have opportunities to develop and use successively higher levels of intellectual ability involving mastery of written and spoken communication. All classroom teachers share the responsibility for developing more abstract levels of thought and communication among their students.

Young adolescents are excited by "thoughtful" classrooms. These classrooms are characterized by the use of stimulating instructional strategies. Students are called on to analyze and synthesize data, to pose questions, to explore, to experiment in explaining their reasoning, and to apply different strategies and solutions to problems posed by their teachers. Coursework assigned to students increasingly challenges them to use the methods of thought and communication which are intrinsic to the various subjects being studied.

Academic achievement rises when students experience thoughtful classrooms. But achieving this goal is complex:

Questions take different forms and place different demands on students. Some questions require only factual recall and do not provoke analysis. For example, of more than 61,000 questions found in teacher guides, student workbooks, and tests for nine history textbooks, more than 95 percent were devoted to factual recall. This is not to say that questions meant to elicit facts are unimportant. Students need basic information to engage in higher level thinking processes and discussions. Such questions also promote class participation and provide a high success rate in answering questions correctly.

Integrated Knowledge and Skills: A Model

In order to become familiar with a work of literature, students might read it to themselves, listen to an audiotape while following the text, or view a filmed or videotaped version. Having gained an understanding of the basic themes, what the students do with that understanding varies in complexity. For instance, one student may write and orally present a brief description of the universality of the themes, using a contemporary film or popular song as an illustration. Taking on a more complex project, another student might conduct an opinion survey of family, friends, school staff, and a few acquaintences in the community by describing a conflict situation in a literary work and asking them what they think might have happened if the main characters had acted differently, and what they would have done in a similar situation. After sorting out, analyzing, graphing, and explaining these opinions to the class and noting their reaction, the student would then write a report of the entire project. Student projects of this type may also be utilized as measures of student achievement.

Janet Kierstead, "Direct Instruction and Experiential Approaches: Are They Really Mutually Exclusive?" *Educational Leadership*. Vol. 42 (May, 1985), pp. 25-30, ©1986. This excerpt was adapted by the author from her original article especially for this report.

factual vs. thought-provoking questions

longer wait (30 secs!) for answers.

The difference between factual and thought-provoking questions is the difference between asking: "When did Lincoln deliver the Gettysburg Address?" and asking: "Why was Lincoln's Gettysburg Address an important speech?" Each kind of question has its place, but the second one intends that the student analyze the speech in terms of the issues of the Civil War.

Although both kinds of questions are important, students achieve more when teachers ask thought-provoking questions and insist on thoughtful answers. Students' answers may also improve if teachers wait longer for a response, giving students more time to think.[1]

Current evidence indicates that the development of critical thinking in the middle grades is far from

1 *What Works: Research About Teaching and Learning.* Prepared under the direction of William J. Bennett. Washington, D.C.: United States Department of Education, 1986, p. 38.

2 Published by permission of Transaction, Inc., from *Successful Schools for Young Adolescents,* by Joan Lipsitz. ©1984 by Transaction, Inc., pp. 189-190.

being a common practice. Lipsitz observes that in middle grade curricula *"the quality of discourse in the classrooms is characterized by a surprising lack of intellectual rigor."*

She adds:

While school administrators stress inquiry into ideas, teachers for the most part stress the transmission of facts. There is relatively little inquiry. The tone of classroom discussion reflects an assumption that young adolescents are developmentally incapable of grappling with concepts.[2]

There is a common misconception that higher order skills must mean advanced skills – the skills you get to after you master the lower order skills. This is not the case. All students think; all stu-

Good Thinking vs. Poor Thinking

This model helps us make some valid and useful distinctions between good and poor thinking. Here we wish to distance ourselves from those who equate good thinking with a long list of discrete mental operations and those who describe poor thinking in terms of several logical errors. ...

Good thinkers are willing to think, and may even find thinking enjoyable. They can carry out searches when necessary and suspend judgment. They value rationality, believing that thinking is useful for solving problems, reaching decisions, and making judgments. Poor thinkers, in contrast, need certainty, avoid thinking, must reach closure quickly, are impulsive, and rely too heavily on intuition.

ASPECT:	THE GOOD THINKER:	THE POOR THINKER:
General Traits	• Welcomes problematic situations and is tolerant of ambiguity.	• Searches for certainty and is intolerant of ambiguity.
	• Is sufficiently self-critical; looks for alternate possibilities and goals; seeks evidence on both sides.	• Is not self-critical and is satisfied with first attempts.
	• Is reflective and deliberative; searches extensively when appropriate.	• Is impulsive, gives up prematurely, and is overconfident of the correctness of initial ideas.
	• Believes in the value of rationality and that thinking can be effective.	• Overvalues intuition, denigrates rationality; believes that thinking won't help.
Goals	• Is deliberative in discovering goals.	• Is impulsive in discovering goals.
	• Revises goals when necessary.	• Does not revise goals.
Possibilities	• Is open to multiple possibilities and considers alternatives.	• Prefers to deal with limited possibilities; does not seek alternatives to an initial possibility.
	• Is deliberative in analyzing possibilities.	• Is impulsive in choosing possibilities.
Evidence	• Uses evidence that challenges favored possibilities.	• Ignores evidence that challenges favored possibilities.
	• Consciously searches for evidence against possibilities that are initially strong, or in favor of those that are weak.	• Consciously searches only for evidence that favors strong possibilities.

higher-order skills
≠
advanced skills

dents can learn ways to think better. No matter how competent students may be or may not be, they must organize their ideas; they must organize their time; they must solve complex problems; and they must think critically.

By emphasizing inquiry into ideas and concepts, young adolescents can engage their imagination directly. This step enables students to make sense out of the vast array of facts with which they are constantly bombarded. Access to ideas and concepts that logically interpret the curriculum must be assured to all students, including those with basic skills deficiencies or limited-English-language proficiency.

Students whose academic experiences uniformly reflect a monotonous daily preoccupation with lower-order intellectual tasks are currently swelling the tide of dropout statistics. These statistics can be tempered through a better instructional balance between emphases on basic skills mastery and the development of more advanced levels of thought.

Arthur Costa suggests that three crucial elements are involved in encouraging the development of thinking skills:

A spirit of inquiry. The classroom where thinking is fostered is one where inquiry is valued. The teacher admits uncertainty: ... "I'm not sure about my interpretation of the poem – I continue to see other things in it." The teacher welcomes intellectual challenges: "You're right in raising that issue – I need to re-think that matter." The teacher also emphasizes education in all subjects as an exploration into the

unknown, as well as teaching what is known. ...

A Teacher's Testimonial

After the inservice on teacher behaviors and their consequences on students' thinking, I decided to test some of the theories in the ... class I teach. I was particularly interested in examining my questioning behaviors and students' responses to them. I was also curious about the effects of silence and nonjudgmental acceptance. When I began the grand experiment, I immediately discovered how difficult it is to structure questions and watch for reactions at the same time.

Given this limitation, I consciously practiced my questioning and response behaviors during a two-week period and began to notice a number of things evolving in the class.

First, the time I spent on lecturing to students declined. There was a shift to a more Socratic format as students became accustomed to processing and applying information. They appeared to become actively involved in what was going on, rather than passively taking notes and listening.

Second, some students who did not participate in class began to join in the discussions. These students seemed to come to an understanding of the material after they had the opportunity to talk about it. The number of "relevant" student questions increased, and students generally began to accept the position that it is not necessary for an answer to be right to be acceptable. More than one answer may solve the same problem.

Third, as I began "accepting" solutions to problems as plausible, more students risked answers. The level of anxiety decreased as students realized their answers wouldn't be classified as either right or wrong. I think that in the process, students were getting much needed practice in using their higher-order cognitive skills.

Finally, I've noticed an increase in test scores on inquiry/application questions. I'm not sure that this increase is due to students becoming more familiar with the test format or to gaining experience in solving these types of questions in class. I hope that it is the latter. Maybe it's a combination of both.

Although this "experiment" in no way reflects the scientific model, it has increased my sensitivity to the need for me to monitor my own behaviors in the classroom. What I do and the manner in which I do it has direct bearing on student behavior and learning.

Ron Edwards, Teacher
Jesuit High School
Sacramento, California

3 Allan A. Glatthorn and Jonathan Barron, "The Good Thinker," in *Developing Minds: A Resource Book for Teaching Thinking.* Edited by Arthur L. Costa. Alexandria, Vir.: Association for Supervision and Curriculum Development, ©1985, p. 52. Reprinted with permission of the Association for Supervision and Curriculum Development. All rights reserved.

An emphasis on problem finding. Most classrooms are places where answers are sought and solutions are valued. *In a thinking-centered classroom, students are taught and encouraged to find problems, to wonder, and to speculate.* ... The teacher nurtures the problem-finding attitude by encouraging students to ask questions, not just answer them: "Here are some data about income distribution in the United States – what questions could we ask?"...

A more deliberative pace. Many classrooms seem to encourage impulsiveness—the teacher asks a question, expects an immediate answer, and calls on the first student who waves a hand. Such rapid-fire recitations are useful in several ways. They facilitate assessment of student knowledge, permit rehearsal of facts, and keep students attentive; yet they can be counterproductive when thinking is the focus. Students need time to deliberate—to reflect about alternate possibilities, to weigh the evidence, and to come to a tentative conclusion....

Whenever possible, examinations should allow time for reflection and discourage guessing. Some students will refuse to learn to think, despite strong encouragement, unless they are convinced that thinking will improve their grades. It is inconsistent to encourage thinking in the classroom and discourage it on tests.[3]

Mastery of reading, writing, speaking, and listening skills becomes increasingly critical for middle grade students precisely because of their relationship to thinking skills. The symbolic languages of mathematics and science and the varied forms of expression characteristic of the visual and performing arts also heighten the power of students to think abstractly and to express themselves in ways which are both creative and logical.

In a directly related context, young adolescents have the growing ability to put together complex concepts and to apply skills across subject matter boundaries. Yet research findings suggest that the middle grade curriculum is too often segmented, compartmentalized, and fragmented. Students do not perceive either implicit or explicit relationships between knowledge and skills gained in one part of the curriculum and those gained in other areas.

Questioning Strategies That Lead to Higher-Level Thinking Skills

The questioning techniques that follow are generally applicable to any questioning model and maximize the potential for a meaningful discussion:

- **Plan key questions to provide lesson structure and direction.** Write them into lesson plans, at least one for each objective – especially higher-level questions. Ask some spontaneous questions based on student responses.

- **Phrase questions clearly and specifically.** Avoid vague or ambiguous questions such as "What did we learn yesterday?" or "What about the heroine of the story?" Ask single questions; avoid run-on questions that lead to student frustration and confusion. Clarity increases probability of accurate responses.

- **Ask questions logically and sequentially.** Avoid random questions lacking clear focus and intent. Consider students' intellectual ability, prior understanding of content, topic, and lesson objective(s). Asking questions in a planned sequence will enhance student thinking and learning.

- **Ask questions at a variety of levels.** Use knowledge-level questions to determine basic understandings and to serve as a basis for higher-level thinking. Higher-level questions provide students opportportunities to practice higher forms of thought.

- **Follow up on student responses.** Develop a response repertoire that encourages students to clarify initial responses, lift thought to higher levels, and support a point of view or opinion. For example, "Can you restate that?" "Could you clarify that further?" "What are some alternatives?" "How can you defend your position?" Encourage students to clarify, expand, or support initial responses to higher-level questions.

Continued on next page

The complexity involved in efforts to integrate multiple subject areas should be recognized. However, middle grade students should experience, at a minimum, an interdisciplinary reading/literature/language arts and/or history/geography core. This core should be taught with a humanities emphasis by one or more teachers in an extended block of instructional time.

Tye effectively presents the case for this recommendation:

The social studies, along with English/language arts, should comprise a minimum core or block-time class…. There are those who would argue for the integration of the arts, science, math and other subjects, as well, into a core. I believe that such total integration is possible, but I also think it takes a very good teacher and that some units of study lend themselves more readily than others to such integration.[4]

Middle grade students require multiple opportunities to perceive conceptual relationships among core curriculum subjects. They need to experience the application of more complex thinking and communicating skills through direct involvement with interdisciplinary curriculums.

Every school should start with a coherent, well-articulated core curriculum for the middle grades. Beyond this core, there should be the ideal of a more complex integration of knowledge and skills. To the degree that this ideal is realized, young adolescents will increasingly be able to conceptualize and to communicate the interrelatedness, symmetry, and beauty of the accumulated knowledge and wisdom of their complex culture.

Continued from previous page

- **Give students time to think when responding.** Increase wait time after asking a question to three to five seconds to increase number and length of student responses and to encourage higher-level thinking. Insisting upon instantaneous responses significantly decreases probability of meaningful interaction with and among students. Allow sufficient wait time before repeating or rephrasing questions to ensure student understanding.

- **Use questions that encourage wide student participation.** Distribute questions to involve the majority of students in learning activities. For example, call on nonvolunteers, using discretion for difficulty level of questions. Be alert for reticent students' verbal and nonverbal cues, such as perplexed look or partially raised hand. Encourage student-to-student interaction. Use circular or semicircular seating to create environment conducive to increased student involvement.

- **Encourage student questions.** This encourages active participation. Student questions at higher cognitive levels stimulate higher levels of thought essential for the inquiry approach. Give students opportunities to formulate questions and carry out followup investigations of interest. Facilitate group and independent inquiry with a supportive social-emotional climate, using praise and encouragement, accepting and applying student ideas, responding to student feelings, and actively promoting student involvement in all phases of learning.

*Essential Questions?
—Key Q's @ beg. of lesson plan.*

4 Kenneth Tye, *The Junior High: A School in Search of a Mission.* Lanham, Md.: University Press of America, Inc., ©1985, p. 326.

TASK FORCE RECOMMENDATIONS

❶ **Local school boards should have middle grade curriculum policies which include the following provisions.**

Recommended policy:

Students in grades 6, 7, and 8 shall receive instruction specifically intended to develop higher order skills in thinking and communicating. This instruction shall be accessible to all students and shall emphasize:

a. **The development of thinking skills which specifically involve moral reasoning, critical thinking, problem solving, aesthetic judgment, and the use of scientific methods**

b. **The development of communication skills characteristic of each subject, including those which specifically involve reading, writing, speaking, and listening; those which involve the nonverbal expressions of the visual and performing arts; and those which involve the symbolic languages of mathematics and science**

❷ **Teachers, teacher trainers, curriculum designers, and publishers should shift the relative allocation of student time from rote tasks toward assignments which call on students to reason and reflect and to communicate their reasoning and reflection through writing, speaking, and other forms of expression. The relative emphasis in graded assignments and tests should shift from simple answers to questions which involve reasoning and problem solving. Students**

Continued on next page

RECOMMENDATIONS *Continued*

should be given feedback on the quality of their reasoning, the scope of their imagination, and their ability to employ knowledge of specific subject matter in solving problems.

❸ The state Legislature should provide funds to local districts which enable middle grade teachers to plan and implement model interdisciplinary programs in the humanities.

Core Curriculum
Interdisciplinary Core
Encourage Higher Order Thinking

Questions!
  ↳ Participation
Reflective Thinking

4 Character Development

Every middle grade student should be helped to personalize ideals and to develop the ability to make reasoned moral and ethical choices.

There is a direct, positive correlation between the ideals for which students strive and the academic success which they experience in school. These ideals include commitment to hard work, personal responsibility, honesty, cooperation, self-discipline, freedom, appreciation of human diversity, and the importance of education itself.

Research findings suggest that students whose parents and friends value education highly tend to have more success and fewer discipline problems in school. Students with a strong sense of traditional ideals use their out-of-school time in ways that reinforce learning. Commitment to hard work and responsibility and to the importance of education have been found to be more important to school success than a student's socioeconomic background.

Such findings argue strongly for the importance of character development as a vital goal of a strong middle grade education program. Conceptually, this goal is hard to define and elusive in terms of attainment because of the inherent sensitivity of moral and ethical issues.

The lure of adolescent pop culture must be balanced by the moral examples set by adults. Students need to confront moral and ethical issues under the guidance of sensitive principals, teachers, and counselors. Two primary goals of middle grade education must be to help students develop their intellectual capacities through reasoned thought and to use this ability in arriving at personal decisions about issues which have moral and ethical consequences.

The study of literature and history, in particular, provide a rich array of possibilities for students as they examine the personal commitments of others to the ideals of hard work, responsibility, and self-improvement. In the same context, these disciplines allow students to encounter literary and historical figures who have had to confront and resolve moral and ethical dilemmas not unlike those which they themselves daily encounter.

While literature and history provide multiple opportunities which

Deeper Meaning

The late teacher-astronaut, Christa McAuliffe, exemplified the type of teacher caught up in the search with her students for the deeper meanings of life's experiences. She likened her pending trip into space to the journey of pioneer women in a Conestoga wagon: "They described things in vivid detail, in word pictures. *They were concerned...with the interaction between people with hopes and fears.* Their diaries are the richest part of the history of our Westward expansion."* She planned to report to students across the nation her own feelings and emotions and to engage them in the excitement of her space odyssey. She saw the need to help students realize the impact of space exploration on their own lives and futures.

Young adolescents are eager to interact with teachers like Christa McAuliffe. They want to learn about the hopes and fears of others just as they want to examine their own. They want teachers who will not shut-down when the conversation shifts toward ultimate questions. They want and need to find the deeper purposes in life.

The Los Angeles Times (January 29, 1986).

can be used to teach and reinforce traditional ideals, all core curriculum subjects have the potential to contribute directly to character development. The social and natural sciences and the arts, for example, are replete with the accounts of individuals whose lives personify commitment, sacrifice, and high accomplishment.

Instructional materials used in the middle grades should include biographies, autobiographies, and other types of resources which reflect the experiences of individuals of widely varying social backgrounds and ethnic origins who have contributed to the basis of our national ideals.

Character development involves more than a definition of moral and ethical principles derived from the lives of significant literary and historical figures. Teachers and counselors must remain involved as students struggle with their own value commitments. This conviction is strengthened by evidence which suggests that students experience the basic development of their adult values during the middle grade years.[1]

One way or another, students will find a way to sort out their deepest longings, thoughts, and feelings. It can happen under the guidance of sensitive, prepared adults who teach and counsel. The alternative may be found in the backwash of the street culture. If this happens, the minds and spirits of many students may be crippled. They will fail to sense that their deepest thoughts and feelings are

respected. The unfolding of their intellects may be compromised and the examples of parents and teachers minimized. Commitments to reality, truth, goodness, and beauty are diminished. Without such commitments any system of personal values becomes dehumanized.

There is a powerful, intrinsic relationship between the development of a mature value system and the capacity to find even partial but essentially positive answers to transcendent questions about the deeper meanings of life. Middle grade students need to be involved in learning tasks that push the edges of their growing abilities to think and to feel. They need to be encouraged to ask about the known, knowable, and unknown dimensions of existence.

Character development should be shared by school personnel with the home and other significant institutions and individuals in each student's life. Principals, teachers, and counselors must be open to the struggles of middle grade students as they confront and seek to resolve issues which ultimately shape the framework of their adult values.

1 *An Agenda for Excellence at the Middle Level.* Reston, Vir.: National Association of Secondary School Principals, 1985, pp. 1-2

The ideals that children hold have important implications for their school experiences. Children who believe in the value of hard work and responsibility and who attach importance to education are likely to have higher academic achievement and fewer disciplinary problems. ... They are also less likely to drop out of school.

What Works: Research About Teaching and Learning.
Prepared under the direction of William J. Bennett. Washington, D.C.: United States Department of Education, 1986, p. 17.

TASK FORCE RECOMMENDATIONS

❶ Teachers, counselors, curriculum leaders, and those who provide their professional training should elevate issues related to the moral and ethical struggles of young adolescents to a much higher level of concern. Attention should be given to the ideals of hard work, personal responsibility, honesty, cooperation, self-discipline, freedom, appreciation of human diversity, and the importance of education. Questions related to reality, truth, goodness, and beauty should be brought to the foreground of studies in the core, elective, and exploratory curricula, including, but not limited to, literature, history, civics, science, and the visual and performing arts. Ways of achieving this goal include:

a. Revisions in curriculum guides and instructional materials which focus attention on the significance of reasoned moral and ethical choices

b. Provision for assignments which involve students in thinking about the moral and ethical struggles of literary and historical personalities and the potential meaning of those experiences in shaping their own ideals

c. Provision of in-service training opportunities for teachers, counselors, and administrators which address ways of responding to the moral and ethical struggles of young adolescents through the content of various core curriculum subjects

Continued on next page

RECOMMENDATIONS *Continued*

② **Principals, teachers, and counselors should demonstrate by example, advice, and instruction the ways in which personal decisions are influenced through moral reasoning based on personal and professional ideals.**

③ **Principals, teachers, counselors, and parents should encourage and guide students to develop a vision of what they hope to be like as adults and to consider how this vision relates to moral and ethical choices which are made during early adolescence. The literary and historical figures and themes found in the varied subjects of the core curriculum, as well as the individual experiences and observations of students themselves, should be employed in addressing this goal.**

5 Learning to Learn

Every middle grade student should develop a repertoire of learning strategies and study skills which emphasizes reflective thought and systematic progression toward the goal of independent learning.

Learning in the lower elementary grades is heavily structured for students by their teachers. In high school, and beyond, students are expected to play a progressively more significant role in structuring their own learning. In the transitional middle grade years, students require instruction in how to learn — how to bridge the distance between highly structured learning environments and those which increasingly move them toward the ideal of independent learners.

Instruction in how to learn is needed in each subject of the core and exploratory curricula. Strategies for approaching and completing assignments are especially critical. These are essential to all future learning and must be emphasized in the middle grades if students are to be successful learners in high school.

Middle grade students have typically matured to the point where they are able to use varied types of learning strategies with increased competence. By the end of grade eight, students should be prepared with a varied repertoire of learning strategies and general study skills. Included in this repertoire should be abilities which enable them to engage in independent study and cooperative learning and to give and receive tutorial instruction.

When major assignments are given in any subject, teachers should help students identify what skills are needed to complete the varied tasks involved. Mastery of new skills, including higher order thinking and communicating skills, should become direct objectives of instruction as students prepare to undertake basic assignments.

For example, teachers can have students:

- State what they expect to achieve by using a specific skill.

Cooperative Learning Groups

To internalize concepts and apply them to new situations, students must interact with materials, express their thoughts, and discuss alternative approaches or explanations. Often, these activities can be accomplished well in groups of four students. Working in small groups increases each student's opportunity to interact with materials and with other students while learning. Students have more chances to speak in a small group than in a class discussion; and in that setting some students are more comfortable speculating, questioning, and explaining concepts in order to clarify their thinking. By brainstorming, exploring various approaches, and solving problems cooperatively, students can gain confidence in their individual abilities.

When a cooperative climate has been established, small groups that are heterogeneous in their composition have the added value of promoting positive attitudes toward others, regardless of individual differences. As a group works together, the differences will be less important than the task at hand. More capable students can assist others. The questions asked by students who do not yet understand an idea will help the entire group to bring its thinking into focus. Individual strengths will be highlighted so that students who have difficulty in some areas will have a chance to contribute their special skills in other areas.

Mathematics Framework for California Public Schools–Kindergarten Through Grade Twelve. Sacramento: California State Department of Education, ©1985, pp. 16-17.

- Describe the procedures and rules they plan to use as they employ the skill.

- Predict the results of their use of the skill.

- Check the procedure they use as they employ the skill.

- Evaluate the outcome of using the skill and the way they employed it.

Such strategies are useful because they allow students to develop a conscious control of their thinking and acting in response to a given assignment. This is a necessary step in learning to learn. The alternative is reliance on a mechanical, low-order repertoire of study skills that do not match the increased academic demands of the core curriculum.

Middle grade students should understand how learning brings about changes in their lives – particularly through those experiences which come from an expanded perception of themselves and their world based on the application of knowledge and skills. This perception empowers students to do creative things, to engage in higher levels of learning, and to explore new categories of knowledge. With this added perspective and the power which it conveys, students can learn to apply themselves increasingly to personal academic goals with long range meaning for their lives.

Students should also be encouraged to approach learning with a direct sense of its more immediate significance. They can be shown that learning to learn is a critical part of their education and that mastery of the skills involved can always be improved .

A sequence of steps, such as the following, is useful in helping students to become increasingly more independent in their learning.

Students can be guided:

1. To look for new information in readings, presentations, and discussions.

2. To look for clues which help to explain the relevance of what is already understood – to surround the new with the background of that which is already familiar.

3. To experiment with what is already known, to search for connections, and to relate previously unrelated information through:
   - Asking questions
   - Defining issues
   - Describing problems and contradictions
   - Formulating hypotheses (educated guesses)
   - Testing hypotheses
   - Preparing and presenting findings and conclusions

4. To note or create patterns and relationships which identify ways of breaking down complex ideas and concepts into manageable components.

5. To develop models and use other strategies to represent patterns and relationships among parts and wholes which bridge

Study Skills: Behaviors Characteristic of Intelligent Action

1. Getting what we need
   - Use our senses (listen, see, smell, taste, and touch) to get information.
   - Use a plan (system) so we do not miss or skip anything important.
   - Give what we do a name.
   - Tell where and when.
   - Tell what stays the same even when things seem to change.
   - Be able to use more than one idea at a time.
   - Be careful when it matters.

2. Using information
   - Know what we are asked to do.
   - Use only the information we need.
   - See a picture in our mind of what we must do.
   - Plan our steps.
   - Keep all the facts in mind.
   - Find out how things go together.
   - Tell what is the same and what is different.
   - Find where things belong.
   - Think things out in our heads — then choose.
   - Prove our ideas.

3. Showing what we know
   - Think before we answer — don't rush.
   - Tell it clearly.
   - If we "know" the answer but can't tell it right away, wait — then try again.
   - Don't panic.

4. We do our best
   - Check to make sure our job is finished.
   - Think about our own thinking.
   - Listen to others tell about their ideas.
   - Tell how we solved the problem.

Arthur L. Costa, "The Behaviors of Intelligence," in *Developing Minds: A Resource Book for Teaching Thinking.* Edited by Arthur L. Costa. Alexandria, Vir.: Association for Supervision and Curriculum Development, ©1985, p. 67. Reprinted with permission of the Association for Supervision and Curriculum Development. All rights reserved.

the gap between existing and new information.

For example, students can prepare:

- Diagrams and charts
- Lists of comparisons and contrasts
- Descriptions of sequences, processes, and causes
- Outlines
- Imaginative stories, scenarios, theories, arguments, and other kinds of explanations and illustrations
- Items which are made and which incorporate two or more ideas or concepts
- Experiments
- Lab reports

6. To play with new information, to explore new combinations of data, and to develop an awareness of the power of concepts and generalizations which unify previously independent facts.

7. To reflect on the ways in which new levels of understanding change perceptions, attitudes, and values.

The learning strategies just described should be accompanied by the acquisition and practice of good study skills. Middle grade students need a strong combination of learning strategies and basic study skills as a necessary foundation for the more demanding and less personalized instructional environment of high school.

Basic study skills include:

- The ability to set study goals and priorities consistent with stated course objectives and one's own progress; to establish surroundings and habits conducive to learning independently or with others; and to follow a schedule that accounts for both short and long-term projects.

- The ability to define, locate, and use resources external to the classroom (for example, library materials, original documents, computer software, interviews, and direct observations) and to combine information gained from such sources with information derived from texts, classroom presentations, and other more conventional sources.

- The ability to develop general and specialized vocabularies and to use them for reading, writing, speaking, listening, computing, and creating.

- The ability to understand and to follow customary instructions for academic work in order to recall, comprehend, analyze, summarize, and report the main ideas from readings, lectures, experiments, and other academic experiences, and to synthesize knowledge and apply it to new situations.

- The ability to prepare for various types of learning assessments and to devise strategies for pacing, attempting, or omitting test questions or thinking, writing, and editing

according to the type of test; and to respond effectively to other types of assessments, such as those represented by projects, class participation, and the evaluations of peers.

- The ability to accept constructive criticism and learn from it.

- The ability to manage time.

The middle grades are a critical point in the development of skills for lifelong learning. The emerging intellectual capacities of young adolescents make the use of more sophisticated learning strategies and study skills possible. Mastery should be seen as a developmental process which receives accelerated attention during the middle grades and which continues into high school and throughout life.

With the rapid growth of peer influence during early adolescence comes the potential for middle grade students to benefit from school practices which are organized around peer-based learning activities. Cooperative learning groups, peer and cross-age tutoring programs, and student study groups have the potential to increase achievement in statistically significant ways. These types of peer-based learning activities help to accomplish three strategic objectives which are critical to early adolescent education:

1. The amount of time available for active participation in the learning process is multiplied. In a group of four, as an example, each participant has the potential

1 *A Nation Prepared: Teachers for the 21st Century.* Washington, D.C.: Carnegie Forum on Education and the Economy, ©1986, p. 47. This report was prepared by the Carnegie Forum on Education and the Economy's Task Force on Teaching as a Profession. The Carnegie Forum is a program of the Carnegie Corporation of New York.

2   Joseph Jenkins and Linda Jenkins, "Peer Tutoring in Elementary and Secondary Programs," *Focus on Exceptional Children,* Vol. 17 (February, 1985), p. 2, ©1985.

to contribute 25 percent of the available discussion. By way of contrast, in a classroom setting involving thirty or more students, only 3 or 4 percent of the discussion time is available to each student.

2. The amount of feedback time for each student is substantially increased, with the potential for affirmation and encouragement to occur more frequently for each individual from within the peer group.

3. The development of positive attitudes toward learning is enhanced as students interact with one another in more tightly focused instructional episodes based on the needs and interests of young adolescents.

Both cooperative learning and peer and cross-age tutoring should be integral components of middle grade classroom instruction. Research evidence suggests that these strategies consistently raise the achievement levels of the students who receive instruction as well as those who provide it.

The Carnegie Corporation, in its recent report, *A Nation Prepared: Teachers for the 21st Century,* provides a scenario which captures the essence of the research on tutorial instruction:

One effort that made a surprisingly big difference ... was the program in which the older students were trained to tutor the younger ones. When many of the older youngsters discovered how superficial their knowledge was when they tried to teach something they thought they knew, they made a real

effort to master the material. They developed a real pride in their ability to help the younger students, and many are going on to become teachers.[1]

After completing an extensive survey of the research literature related to tutorial instruction, Jenkins and Jenkins conclude:

If teachers desire to increase academic engaged time through one-to-one instruction, they must expand their reserve of instructional personnel. They need not look far. Some of the best helpers are other students who can be recruited from inside their own school.[2]

Peer helper programs reach out to a wide variety of students, and those who tutor should reflect the same diversity. Good programs encourage participation by average students as well as the stars and by those who represent every ethnic and linguistic background or socio-economic circumstance. Physically handicapped students, those with limited English proficiency, the gifted, those who are at-risk — in short, every student is a candidate for a peer or cross-age tutor role. The genius of peer helper programs is found in the fact that the reservoir of talent is almost limitless.

Administrators are attracted to peer tutoring by its cost effectiveness. Research undertaken by the Institute on Educational Finance and Governance at Stanford is summarized by Michael Kirst, former president of the California State Board of Education:

To respect the limitations on public funding means giving careful attention to the relative costs of educational improvements. An evaluation of four different strategies for improvement *has revealed significant differences in cost. The four strategies are these: (1) reducing class size by adding more teachers, (2) increasing the length of the school day, (3) using computers to facilitate instruction, and (4) providing tutors – peer or adult. A study measured the gain in pupils' achievement scores in reading and mathematics purchased by $300 in funding for each approach. In general, peer tutoring proved the most cost-effective, and reducing class size and increasing the length of the school day the least cost-effective. Computer-assisted instruction ranked between these extremes.[3]*

Peer tutoring also provides a more caring school climate. Students who invest in each others' successes experience a sense of personal satisfaction as well as achievement.

There is another dimension of peer and cross-age tutoring which is highly significant. The potential for interesting students in teaching careers is ever present. Underrepresented minorities in particular may find that peer tutoring leads to exciting career options.

The Carnegie Report argues the case persuasively:

One particularly promising development is the use on a large scale of ... students to work as tutors in schools with high concentrations of low-income students. When both tutor and taught are minority students, both will benefit. Furthermore, minority ... students who serve as tutors may find that they enjoy teaching sufficiently to make teaching their career choice, turning such programs into a recruiting device as well.[4]

Cooperative learning and one-to-one tutoring using peer and cross-age student volunteers should be implemented in every school serving the middle grades. These in-structional strategies are cost-effective, increase learning, and are directly consistent with the middle grade philosophy which stresses a personal concern for all students.

A direct corollary of learning strategies, study skills, cooperative learning, and peer tutorial programs is the special role of homework. In effect, sound homework policies have the ability to extend the regular classroom experiences of students in significant ways and to reinforce all other efforts aimed at developing independent learners.

Increased reliance on the use of homework during the middle grades reflects the growing capacity of young adolescents to take responsibility for their own learning. This includes a deliberate recognition of the need to prepare for the homework demands of high school as well.

Sound homework policies provide students with the opportunity to carry out assignments

3 Michael W. Kirst, *Who Controls Our Schools?* Stanford, Calif.: Stanford Alumni Association, ©1984, p. 158.

4 *A Nation Prepared: Teachers for the 21st Century.* Washington, D.C.: Carnegie Forum on Education and the Economy, ©1986, p. 84. This report was prepared by the Carnegie Forum on Education and the Economy's Task Force on Teaching as a Profession. The Carnegie Forum is a program of the Carnegie Corporation of New York.

The Allendale School Tutorial Program

Student tutors are recommended by their teachers on the basis of responsibility, conscientiousness, and reliability. During four training sessions, tutors learn their responsibilities, positive tutor behavior, and the content of their "skill-based" reading and math tutoring units. Tutors and tutees are matched on a one-to-one basis for the entire year. Tutoring sessions range form thirty minutes twice a week to thirty or forty minutes five times a week. Tutors meet once per month to share insights and problems. At least twice per month, the trainer meets individually with each tutor to discuss the progress of the tutee. A network of referrals among tutor, teacher, and trainer kept everyone working together. Thorough written evaluations take place at the end of the year. The program changes, grows, and improves each year.

Cynthia Harris
Coordinator, Staff Development
Oakland Unified School District

5 *What Works: Research About Teaching and Learning.* Prepared under the direction of William J. Bennett. Washington, D.C.: United States Department of Education, 1986, p. 42.

6 James J. Fenwick, *The Middle School Years.* San Diego, Calif.: Fenwick Associates, ©1986, p. 17.

independently according to clear directions and the prior learning of essential study skills. These skills must include the capacity to determine the relative importance of different aspects of the assigned work. Homework should include assignments which arouse curiosity, raise questions for further exploration, and foster the self-discipline required for independent study.

Homework assignments should also give students the chance to try out in practical ways the things which they are learning in the classroom. Students need opportunities to explore and experiment with new understandings and skills. This can occur through highly structured homework given by the teacher. Or, as students become more competent and responsible, the structure of their assignments can become largely a product of their own planning in consultation with their teachers.

The relative value of homework is directly related to the clarity of directions, expectations, and time lines communicated to students by teachers and the immediacy and clarity of the feedback which students receive following completion of their work. Homework is most productive when students are given a sense of the understandings and skills they are expected to employ in completing assignments and the knowledge base which is to be used:

To make the most of what students learn from doing homework, teachers need to give the same care to preparing homework assignments as they give to classroom instruction. When teachers prepare written instructions and discuss homework assignments with students, they find their students take the homework more seriously than if the assignments are simply announced. Students are more willing to do homework when they believe it is useful, when teachers treat it as an integral part of instruction, when it is evaluated by the teacher, and when it counts as a part of the grade.

Assignments that require students to think, and are therefore more interesting, foster their desire to learn both in and out of school. Such activities include explaining what is seen or read in class; comparing, relating, and experimenting with ideas; and analyzing principles.[5]

But homework cannot fill the void if students fail to have the opportunity to think about their curricula and to communicate with each other in the classroom about their independent assignments. When this opportunity exists, then homework becomes a natural extension of the classroom:

Regular, consistent, sensible homework is one of the best ways to extend a student's educational experiences without new investments of tax dollars. But a warning is needed. "More is not necessarily better." Homework should not be defined by meaningless, repetitious drill and practice exercises. The ideal homework assignment reinforces concepts previously taught in the classroom and is fitted to the environment of the home... A good book to read, a short essay to write, or a series of problems to solve – all lend themselves to tasks which parents can successfully monitor, even if they do not understand all the implications of a given assignment.[6]

The National Assessment of Educational Progress (NAEP) reports that in 1985, 25 percent of eighth grade students watched television at least five hours per day. Arthur Berger, in his book, *The TV Guided American*, points out that by the time average young persons reach eighteen years of age, they have seen 22,000 hours of programs and 600,000 commercials totaling three years of their lives. Parents and teachers must confront this head-on competition between homework and television and co-opt the latter for curriculum and instructional purposes whenever possible.

Local district superintendents, school principals, and teachers share a primary responsibility in coordinating communications with parents regarding homework policies. In some communities the attainment of homework goals may be extremely hard to achieve. Continuous, deliberate attempts to communicate between the school and the home regarding the purposes of homework and the expected parental support involved have the potential to benefit students in critical ways.

It is essential to put the issue of homework in perspective relative to other demands on the time and energy of teachers. A significant amount of time and effort is involved in effectively and conscientiously planning, differentiating, monitoring, and evaluating homework assignments. Teachers who systematically spend added hours daily on these tasks should receive professional incentives. School boards should realistically evaluate the quality and value of homework in the middle grades. Homework

Television Viewing: Guidelines for the Middle Grades

- Involve students in discussion about the role and influence of television in society; stress the tendency of those who control program content to dramatize and glamorize the sensational in order to capture the viewer's interest; help students evaluate the meaning and consequence of these factors for themselves, as viewers;

- Selectively assign television programs as adjuncts to regular classroom assignments;

- Choose program content that has the ability to stimulate independent thought including documentaries about nature, geography, technology, and world events;

- Include viewing assignments that introduce students to the visual and performing arts;

- Have guided classroom discussions about what has been seen, heard, felt, and thought in relation to specific viewing assignments;

- Have frank talks with students about television addiction and its power to compromise their minds, emotions and effective use of personal time;

- Communicate with parents about the school's attempts to use television constructively to augment classroom learning;

- Help parents confront the responsibility to involve their children in talking about the ways in which television can get out of control and thereby damage family relationships;

- Provide parents with guidelines or other information to help them monitor the amount and type of viewing which their children experience;

- Encourage students and parents to watch some programs together and to then talk about what they have seen and heard; for example, typical conversations might include:

  - What were the issues expressed in this program? Were there morals?

  - What kinds of choices or options were possible in response to the issues?

  - What might have been the consequences of each of these choices or optional responses?

  - Would each of you (parent and student) have chosen to respond in the same way as the main characters in the program (fictional or nonfictional)? If so, why? If not, why not?

James J. Fenwick, *The Middle School Years.* San Diego, Calif.: Fenwick Associates, ©1986, p. 19.

policies should be defined which have substance and which reward teachers who provide evidence that these policies are regularly and creatively implemented.

Learning to learn involves multiple instructional emphases. Cooperative learning, peer and cross-age tutoring, mastery of generalized and specialized study skills and learning strategies, and sound homework practices represent some of the most important classroom priorities as young adolescents are helped to move toward the goal of independent learning. Middle grade education should emphasize each of these priorities for all students in the regular instructional program.

TASK FORCE RECOMMENDATIONS

1 Local school boards should have middle grade curriculum policies which ensure that all students have the opportunity:

  a. To develop a repertoire of generalized learning strategies and study skills (including test-taking skills)

  b. To develop particularized learning strategies and study skills unique to the special requirements of specific subjects

  c. To participate in cooperative learning and peer/cross-age tutoring programs

2 The California State Department of Education should ensure that the frameworks and *Model Curriculum Guides (K– 8)* give explicit attention to the development of study skills – particularly those needed to complete more complex tasks typical of each subject area in the core curriculum.

3 Textbook publishers should be required to emphasize explicitly the conscious, reflective aspects of independent learning in texts adopted for use in the middle grades.

Continued on next page

RECOMMENDATIONS *Continued*

④ **Teachers should help students develop learning strategies required to cope with increasingly more challenging instructional materials, including those which help to prepare students for success in high school curricula.**

⑤ **Local school boards should adopt policies and allocate resources to enable schools which enroll students in the middle grades to establish cooperative learning groups and peer/cross-age tutoring programs.**

⑥ **The State Department of Education should provide advice to local districts, including models and strategies needed to assist middle grade schools in establishing cooperative learning groups and peer/cross-age tutoring programs.**

⑦ **Teachers should assign homework as an extension of an active learning classroom environment; homework assignments should focus on the goals of the core curriculum; and particular attention should be given to assignments which incorporate reading and writing skills.**

⑧ **School boards should define a middle grade homework policy. A general guideline for teachers, students, and parents should be a range of eight to twelve hours of homework per week. (Note: The qualitative aspects of homework assignments should receive priority emphasis. The quantity and quality of homework cannot be measured directly by the time spent since different students will spend different amounts of time on the same assignment.)**

Continued on next page

RECOMMENDATIONS *Continued*

⑨ School boards should provide incentives to teachers who consistently invest substantial amounts of additional professional time, apart from the classroom, in planning, differentiating, monitoring, and evaluating homework assignments.

⑩ Principals, teachers, and parents should creatively address the conflict between homework and television viewing. Teachers should use television as an adjunct of the curriculum when appropriate and should assist parents in guiding their children's viewing habits.

⑪ Local school boards should evaluate middle grade teaching loads; consideration should be given to specialized roles and responsibilities; and adjustments in teaching loads should be made, when required, in keeping with district commitments to the goals of middle grade education reform.

6 Instructional Practice

Instructional practice should emphasize active learning strategies which are consistent with the goals of the core curriculum and the developmental characteristics of young adolescents.

Instructional practices in the middle grades should join young adolescents to the core, elective, and exploratory curricula. In order to be successful, instructional practices must be appropriate to the structure and substance of varied subjects and the developmental characteristics of students. These two conditions must be met. When either is missing, the connection is broken between students and the curricula; the primary mission of the school is compromised.

The characteristics of young adolescents are too often interpreted as obstacles to learning. When this happens, instructional practices can fight the restless energy, fascination with peer culture norms, and curiosity about themselves and their world which are typical of middle grade students. The consequences can be destructive – even tragic – in terms of wasted human lives.

The curricula recommended by the California State Department of Education *(Model Curriculum Guides)*, as well as the recommendations of professional curriculum organizations, stress the importance of systematically empowering students to do for themselves whatever each subject requires – in other words, enabling them to move toward the ideal of independent learners. *Active learning* instructional strategies become very important at this point. This type of learning involves students intellectually and physically in varied learning tasks. This occurs with differing levels of direction, guidance, and feedback from teachers. Active learning is contrasted to passive learning in which exposition involving one–way communication between teachers and students is the dominant instructional style.

Active learning strategies possess the potential to respond to both the wide diversity of student learning styles and the individual

---

Neither Commitment nor Comprehension...

...while students clamor for task simplicity and clarity, they frequently report that school work is boring and tedious. As academic tasks become more routinized and removed from children's lives, the applicability and meaning they do possess are obscured (Goodlad, 1983). Although children may feel more secure when completing simple tasks, their motivation to engage meaningfully in these tasks may well decline. Moreover, the repetition of simplified task forms like worksheets may diminish student interest in the content itself since children may not distinguish between the form of the task and its content. After several years, the sameness of task forms may render the subject matter content itself uninteresting.

...in the long term, the cumulative experience of unvaried, simple task content and forms produces students who are limited thinkers and alienated workers. Many students merely tolerate schoolwork and express neither commitment to, nor comprehension of, the learning goals enunciated by teachers. We speculate that this may result largely from the experience of a restricted range of tasks. Even when students perceive they are able and can succeed, they are unlikely to function in and out of the classroom as creative thinkers and motivated workers if the task forms they have experienced are boring and the content simplistic.

Phyllis C. Blumenfeld, John R. Mergendoller, and Donald W. Swarthout, "Task as a Heuristic for Understanding Student Learning and Motivation," *Journal of Curriculum Studies*, Vol. 19, No. 2 (1987), p. 144, ©1987, Taylor & Francis Ltd. Used by permission of the publisher.

strengths of teachers. They involve substantive changes in the way both students and teachers work together:

The students ... must be active learners, busily engaged in the process of bringing new knowledge and new ways of knowing to bear on a widening range of increasingly difficult problems. The focus of schooling must shift from teaching to learning, from the passive acquisition of facts and routines to the active application of ideas to problems. That transition makes the role of the teacher more important, not less.[1]

Students learn by doing. They learn from seeking answers to questions that have stimulated their imaginations. There should be many opportunities both inside and outside the classroom to look for answers, to test hypotheses, and to reach tentative conclusions.

Middle grade students are especially responsive to combinations of tactile, auditory, and/or visual instructional modes. All learners need to have ample opportunity for hands-on activities. Many students will not learn well if forced to rely solely on one instructional strategy:

Many students have misconceptions even after taking a science course because they have not had opportunities to test and witness the evidence that would change their minds. To clear up misconceptions, students need to be given the chance to predict the results they anticipate in an experiment. For example, the mistaken idea that the basketball will fall faster than the ping-pong ball can be tested experimentally. The teacher can then explain why the original hypothesis was faulty. In this way experiments help students use the scientific method to distinguish facts from opinions and misconceptions.[2]

Students learn by exploring multiple sources of written information, including library references, collateral texts, original documents, or other similar resources. Their ability to do more abstract thinking gives them the capacity to use research skills to find answers available to them through their own efforts.

Young adolescents are seeking answers to life's ultimate questions. Who am I? Why am I here? What is real, true, good, beautiful? Their search is paralleled by the central themes of literature, history, the arts, and other disciplines. These are the themes which must be emphasized in the core curriculum for the middle grades.

The use of questions about the deeper issues of life as a point of entry into the humanities and social studies curricula has profound implications for instructional practice. Questioning techniques encourage and provoke students to think, to organize their thoughts, and to reach conclusions based on reason and evidence.

For every student to have enough experiences of this type requires questioning strategies that incorporate critical elements of Socratic dialogue. Teachers must clearly phrase questions and then allow sufficient waiting time for all students to prepare their thoughts with a clear expectation of being called upon to respond.

The use of small groups within a class multiplies by several fold the opportunity of each student to respond to questions. Students

1 *A Nation Prepared: Teachers for the 21st Century.* Washington, D.C.: Carnegie Forum on Education and the Economy, ©1986, p. 25. This report was prepared by the Carnegie Forum on Education and the Economy's Task Force on Teaching as a Profession. The Carnegie Forum is a program of the Carnegie Corporation of New York.

2 *What Works: Research About Teaching and Learning.* Prepared under the direction of William J. Bennett. Washington, D.C.: United States Department of Education, 1986, p. 23.

who are taught what to look for in the responses of others and how to give each other good critiques experience an increased frequency and higher quality of feedback vital to the effective use of this instructional practice.

Variations in questioning strategies are needed as teachers make open-ended, probing inquiries designed to encourage their students to engage in thoughtful, active learning. These variations are particularly appropriate for mathematics and science. Teaching for understanding and problem solving is the growing emphasis in mathematics. (See *Mathematics Framework* and *Model Curriculum Guide: Mathematics*). Students with varied skill levels are asked, for instance, to construct mathematical ideas in relation to a variety of imaginative situations. The roles of teachers transcend those of suppliers of answers and "recipes" for concocting answers. Rather, teachers are asked to draw out the reasoning processes of students and to stimulate their mathematical imaginations.

A parallel opportunity exists in science. The *Science Framework Addendum* and the *Model Curriculum Guide: Science* stress the importance of understanding scientific concepts and their supportive evidence as well as the processes which have led to given conclusions. These processes begin with curiosity and wonder about the world – qualities particularly characteristic of young adolescents. Out of curiosity and wonder come the impetus to question, to observe, to hypothesize, and to experiment – the essential ingredients needed to develop scientific theories.

The way scientists discover and accumulate scientific knowledge should be paralleled by the way in which middle grade students build their own knowledge base. The various scientific processes provide a powerful source of active instructional strategies for teaching and learning science as well as other disciplines in the core, elective, and exploratory curricula.

The middle grade curricula should stretch the minds of students. Young adolescents have the capacity to learn to use increasingly complex mental processes. Instructional practices must be used which enhance their capacity to master these processes. Evidence indicates that this does not happen systematically in the typical middle

Questioning Strategies Which Encourage the Development of a "Thoughtful Classroom"

When teachers rely on questions with short, correct answers and call on students with their hands raised, they are encouraging recall in some students and ignoring others entirely. In contrast, teachers should:

- Ask questions which have a range of appropriate responses, all of which require some explanation of the student's thinking;
- Wait 5 to 10 seconds for all students to think, and then;
- Call on students without anyone raising hands.

By doing this, several important purposes are accomplished:

- All students know they are expected to think;
- They are given the time and silence to think;
- All students must be ready to communicate their thoughts.

grade classroom. The allocation of instructional time should be such that the more complex learning outcomes receive proper attention.

To accomplish this goal, teachers should:

- Establish clearly stated learning outcomes which involve a balance between more limited and more complex cognitive skills; they should make sure that the purposes of these outcomes are fully understood by students.

- Present a sequence of well-organized learning activities that are specifically related to these outcomes.

- Employ clear, precise explanations, illustrations, or other appropriate techniques to teach skills, content, and/or processes.

- Ask questions frequently or use other pertinent strategies to see if assignments are understood and if learning outcomes have been attained.

- Provide multiple opportunities for students to practice basic skills and to apply and extend them to new situations.

Individual and/or joint student projects should be major features of each unit of study in core curriculum subjects. These projects provide students with learning experiences which allow them to draw on the most important ideas, concepts, and skills gained from their studies. These projects should reflect what a culturally literate adult is able to do in our society so that students become prepared to assume that role.

Projects provide many other important advantages for middle grade students. For example:

- Projects can be designed to focus on more complex, higher order learning which enables ideas and concepts to be integrated in order to achieve a synergistic learning effect.

- Projects provide a valuable alternative means to evaluate student learning which offsets some of the limitations of paper/pencil tests.

A Model for Linking Traditional Direct Instruction and More Complex Thinking Processes

Various instructional strategies can be employed to develop higher order thinking processes. These strategies create an optimum balance between the basic skills developed through traditional direct instruction and more complex thought developed through experiential approaches. Content is developed through connecting "units" of study. A unit may begin with the presentation of information to the total group, but the teacher may then use other instructional strategies such as cooperative learning, discovery, inquiry, etc., and separate students into smaller groups. Students use computers, calculators, video equipment, and other technology. They also use concrete materials on a regular basis (e.g. unifix cubes, scales, other lab equipment, three-dimensional models, etc.) Skills and concepts gained through such learning experiences are then applied and extended through student projects. These projects give students the opportunity to create something of interest to them: a three-dimensional model, a mural, skit, commercial, mock TV documentary, etc. One unit of study builds on the next; content unfolds logically and process — what the students are expected to do with that content — increases in complexity.

Janet Kierstead, "Direct Instruction and Experiential Approaches: Are They Really Mutually Exclusive?" *Educational Leadership.* Vol. 42, (May, 1985), pp. 25-30, ©1985. This excerpt was adapted by the author from her original article especially for this report.

- Projects provide structure for classroom management which allows for true individualization of instruction; teachers interact independently with students as they develop specific skills.

- Projects help to teach middle grade students the kinds of self-management skills needed in high school, in higher education, and on the job.

- Projects allow adjustment to differences in learning styles and skill levels and allow a broad range of students to experience success in accomplishing interesting, challenging assignments.

- Projects allow time lines which are less vulnerable to student absences which compromise short-cycle, cumulatively sequenced curriculum designs.

- Projects exemplify the importance of learning to students, parents, and the community in ways which are immediate, tangible, meaningful, and convincing.

Managing instruction for active learning requires a variety of classroom settings. Frequently, students in small groups, pairs, or individually will be working on projects, engaging in discussions, experimenting with ideas and concepts, dialoging, debating issues, developing hypotheses, solving problems, creating models, planning presen-

Managing Instructional Time

Effective time managers in the classroom do not waste valuable minutes on unimportant activities; they keep their students continuously and actively engaged. Good managers perform the following time-conserving functions:

- Planning Class Work: choosing the content to be studied, scheduling time for presentation and study, and choosing those instructional activities (such as grouping, seatwork, or recitation) best suited to learning the material at hand;

- Communicating Goals: setting and conveying expectations so students know what they are to do, what it will take to get a passing grade, and what the consequences of failure will be;

- Regulating Learning Activities: sequencing course content so knowledge builds on itself, pacing instruction so students are prepared for the next step, monitoring success rates so all students stay productively engaged regardless of how quickly they learn, and running an orderly, academically focused classroom that keeps wasted time and misbehavior to a minimum.

When teachers carry out these functions successfully and supplement them with a well-designed and well-managed program of homework, they can achieve three important goals:

- They capture students' attention.

- They make the best use of available learning time.

- They encourage academic achievement.

What Works: Research About Teaching and Learning. Prepared under the direction of William J. Bennett. Washington, D.C.: United States Department of Education, 1986, p. 34.

tations, or otherwise engaging in active learning tasks.

Teachers must increasingly share instructional management responsibilities with students during the middle grades. This is essential if students are to be allowed to learn to take part successfully in the active learning strategies just described. Necessary skills include cooperative learning techniques, group discussion strategies, time management skills, problem solving methods, and simple project management practices.

Middle grade students are able to achieve – even master – significant levels of competence related to each of these abilities. They can and want to respond to planned, systematic, incremental increases in their own responsibility for independent learning. At the same time, their teachers must continue to monitor and guide their progress

3 *What Works: Research About Teaching and Learning.* Prepared under the direction of William J. Bennett. Washington, D.C.: United States Department of Education, 1986, p. 32.

toward this goal. The ideal is found in a shared responsibility for managing instruction by teachers and students. Students who enter the ninth grade with a background of active learning experiences will be better prepared to handle high school curricula and to succeed in the less personalized learning environment which they are likely to encounter in secondary classrooms.

Minority students are often the least likely to have access to the benefits of active learning in the middle grades. They are frequently the victims of low expectations – their own as well as those of the significant adults in their lives. If expectations for any student are compromised, the curriculum is violated. Diminished expectations typically relegate affected students to low-order skill mastery or rote recall. Students rarely if ever experience the power of their minds which the core curriculum is designed to elicit:

Students from whom teachers expect less are treated differently. Such students typically:

- *Are seated farther away from the teacher,*
- *Receive less direct instruction,*
- *Have fewer opportunities to learn new material, and*
- *Are asked to do less work.*

Teachers also call on these students less often, and the questions they ask are more likely to be simple and basic than thought-provoking. Typically, such students are given less time to respond and less help when their answers are wrong. But when teachers give these same students the chance to answer more challenging questions, the students contribute more ideas and opinions to class discussions.[3]

Instructional Materials: Quality and Quantity

The existing state fund, and the formula for distributing it to local districts are both woefully inadequate. Basic unit costs have risen. The cost of an average science textbook today is $17 each, yet the entire appropriation for materials per student per year in secondary schools is only $12 - not enough to pay for a single science textbook. And schools need more varied and advanced materials to increase the productivity of teachers facing larger and larger classes. Supplementary materials such as maps, globes, workbooks, simulations, software, and video equipment are no longer luxuries, but necessities which schools lack the funds to procure.

The California Commission on the Teaching Profession surveyed California teachers and discovered that:

- One-quarter of teachers surveyed reported they do not have a textbook for every student.

- One-quarter report they do not have the other, non-textbook, basic learning materials they need. In fact, 38 percent spend more than $100 of their own money each year on classroom materials, rather than simply go without.

- One-fifth report they do not have access to the audio-visual equipment they need.

Once again, California compares poorly with other states. In a separate, national survey, 52 percent of the California teachers reported inadequate supplies, materials, and facilities, compared with 36 percent nationwide. And 62 percent of California teachers reported overcrowded classes, compared with 46 percent nationwide.

Who Will Teach Our Children? A Strategy for Improving California's Schools. Sacramento: The California Commission on the Teaching Profession, 1985, p. 28.

All middle grade students should be intellectually challenged through the use of multiple instructional strategies. Classrooms cannot be divided between the academic "haves" and "have nots." For the latter, learning becomes disconnected, episodic, and low in both quality and content. Instructional strategies must be exciting, pertinent, integrated, and diverse. There is a special urgency about this need because the middle grades represent for multitudes of youth the turning point with respect to their lifelong academic interest and commitment.

Active learning strategies also have implications for the instructional materials which middle grade students require. In many classrooms there is an overreliance on textbooks and other materials designed and written by educators. More emphasis should be given to materials written, designed, or edited by professionals within the discipline being studied. Paperback fiction and nonfiction should supplement textbooks as a necessary part of the instructional materials repertoire needed in literature, history, and other areas of the core curriculum.

New instructional technologies should be used wherever appropriate in teaching middle grade learners. Video cassettes and VCRs, compact discs, hand calculators, microcomputers, and software programs represent only a small sample of the technology increasingly available to teachers and students.

Sharing Responsibility with Students in the Active Learning Setting

While allowing students to operate independently through planning the use of their own time and by making decisions regarding pace, sequence, and content of their projects, the teacher never fully relinquishes control. Instead, the teacher establishes a set of rules, routines, and consequences which make it possible to monitor and guide what students are doing. For example, students are taught to follow a procedure which looks something like the following:

1. **Gather materials and equipment:** They begin by gathering what they need to carry out their work. These resources are usually kept in a pre-established location, within easy reach of the students, so that they do not waste time searching for them or waiting for them to be handed out.

2. **Carry out the task:** Students know what is expected of them as they work:

   They understand rules for general behavior such as where they may sit, how much talking and walking about is acceptable, and whether they may work with other students.

   Standards for the quality, quantity, and complexity of work have been established.

   They know where and how to get help. Peer tutors or a student "buddy system" encourage them to share information and ideas with fellow students.

3. **Have work checked and signed off:** Students are responsible for asking the teacher to check and sign off on their work upon completion of all or a pre-determined portion of a project. At this point, they receive specific feedback and may be required to make a correction or expand the work and then return for another check before the teacher completely signs off on it.

4. **Record that work is complete:** Once the teacher has made the final check, the student indicates by a visual signal (usually by checking off on a class chart) that his or her task is complete. This allows the teacher to see, at a glance, how far each student has progressed during the project period.

5. **Turn in completed work:** Students usually place completed work in a central location so the teacher can look through it outside of class time. This allows the teacher to assess student work and plan which students should receive special attention during the next project period.

6. **Return materials and equipment:** Students know how to care for and return materials and equipment to storage areas so that they remain in good condition.

7. **Begin another activity:** The student knows what to do once the first portion of a project is complete.

Janet Kierstead, "How Teachers Manage Individual and Small-Group Work in Active Classrooms," *Educational Leadership,* Vol. 44 (October, 1986), p. 23, ©1986. This excerpt was adapted by the author from her original article especially for this report.

For example:

[students can] ... use microcomputers to write competent essays and produce computer animated art. One inner-city elementary school's students are learning basic engineering principles as they design and build computer-controlled experiments. Middle school students are learning the principles of advanced mathematics as they write programs to create complex geometric shapes. High school students are learning how to use spreadsheet software designed for business to optimize feeding schedules for individual dairy cows on their family farms, thereby achieving efficiencies that have eluded their parents.

Currently available software also makes it possible for music students to compose, edit, and play music for multiple instruments. Science students can set up remote data-gathering stations and connect them to microcomputers to forecast the weather in remote mountain valleys, learning both about the science of weather forecasting and the principles of computer-based modeling....

None of the subjects is taught by the computer, but the computer is used by the student as a tool to accomplish these tasks. The result is that students of all ability levels can learn much more, and learn it earlier in their school career.

Video recorders and laser disk players are now available that can bring large amounts of information to individual students on demand, including high quality visual images.[4]

New instructional strategies and state of the art technology can create a level of vulnerablility for students and teachers alike. Young adolescents are extremely sensitive to the risk of embarassing themselves. A school culture which encourages "intellectual risks," including the probability of frequent mistakes, is essential in the middle grades.

Faculty members must model the capacity to learn through risking and to respond to mistakes in a mature manner, including the ability to laugh at themselves. The joy — and humor — of learning should be viewed as a corollary of serious academic purpose. These qualities should become significant personal insights gained by students in the middle grades.

4 *A Nation Prepared: Teachers for the 21st Century.* Washington, D.C.: Carnegie Forum on Education and the Economy, ©1986, p. 94. This report was prepared by the Carnegie Forum on Education and the Economy's Task Force on Teaching as a Profession. The Carnegie Forum is a program of the Carnegie Corporation of New York.

TASK FORCE RECOMMENDATIONS

① **Local school boards should have middle grade curriculum policies which include the following provisions.**

Recommended policy:

Instructional practices for grades 6, 7, and 8 shall emphasize learning activities which further the goals of the core curriculum and which reflect the development characteristics of early adolescent students. In addition to sound instructional practices which are generalizable to all grade levels, priority shall be given in grades 6, 7, and 8 to active learning strategies and the progressive development of student responsibility for managing learning assignments. These goals shall be attained through:

a. *Thoughtful Classrooms*

Questioning strategies shall be used which encourage students to think and to communicate their thoughts; large- and small-group activities shall be employed to facilitate opportunities for students to share their reasoning with others; these activities shall emphasize the use of thinking skills which transcend simple recall and personal opinion; and time to think shall be provided for all students before and during their responses when questioning strategies are used in the classroom.

b. *Student Projects*

In each core curriculum subject the most important instructional objectives at each grade level shall be taught, in part, through student projects. Projects shall be

Continued on next page

RECOMMENDATIONS *Continued*

designed to enable students to apply skills and to use facts, ideas, concepts, and generalizations in addressing issues and problems related to central themes of the subject; when two or more subjects are taught in a core curriculum instructional block, projects shall be designed which have the potential to integrate skills and knowledge through addressing interdisciplinary themes.

c. *Responsibility for Learning*

Students shall receive direct instruction on how to manage their individual learning activities; they shall be given progressively more personal responsibility and accountability for organizing and completing their assignments.

d. *Enjoyment of Learning*

Students shall be helped to experience the joy and rewards associated with academic commitment and individual achievement. They shall be encouraged to risk intellectually in the process of learning and be helped to accept mistakes which accompany trial and error as a necessary part of their learning experiences. They shall be helped to learn in a classroom atmosphere which values patience and humor as essential qualities of successful learners.

e. *Instructional Materials*

Textbooks shall be supplemented by the use of fiction and nonfiction paperbacks, library resources, teacher and student-made materials, software, films and video

Continued on next page

RECOMMENDATIONS *Continued*

cassettes, laboratory and studio supplies and equipment, and community resources, as appropriate to the curriculum. The selection and use of instructional materials shall be determined by the learning activity and the subject matter; choices of instructional materials shall represent those most likely to engage young adolescents actively in their pursuit of major curriculum objectives; allocations of instructional materials funds shall be based on the requirements of specified learning activities.

② The faculty in each school which enrolls students in the middle grades should:

a. Study:

- The middle grade curriculum recommended by the State Department of Education in its *Model Curriculum Guides*

- The principles, discussions, and recommendations related to middle grade curriculum and instruction contained in this report

- The recommendations of curriculum associations and other respected professional sources related to middle grade education

- The middle grade goals and policies of their respective districts

b. Establish priorities for improvements in middle grade curriculum and instruction. These priorities should be communicated to district administrators with requests for assistance and support, as required.

Continued on next page

RECOMMENDATIONS *Continued*

❸ **Faculties should employ strategies for achieving middle grade curriculum and instructional improvements which include, but are not limited to:**

a. Continuous commitment to collegial support, which includes common planning time, visits to other classrooms, peer coaching, and other practices which emphasize mutual support and recognition

b. Shared convictions among students, administrators, teachers, and counselors relative to the importance of "thoughtful classrooms" in which instructional practices enhance the development and use of higher order thinking skills

c. Agreement by faculty members on priority core curriculum objectives which become the basis for major student projects common to each middle grade level in each subject; emphasis shall be given to interdisciplinary projects whenever appropriate

d. Employment of educational practices which improve opportunities for successful learning experiences in the core curriculum for students historically diverted to less demanding curricula

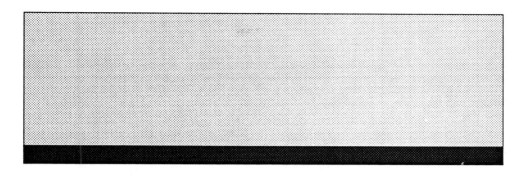

PART TWO

STUDENT POTENTIAL:

Realizing the "Highest and Best"
Intellectual, Social, Emotional,
and Physical Development

7 Academic Counseling

Every middle grade student should have timely information about the relationship between the curricula of the middle and secondary grades and should be provided access to the opportunity to prepare for the broadest possible range of academic options (curriculum paths) in high school.

Academic counseling should be provided through a planned procedure which ensures that middle grade students have timely access to critical information about the school curriculum and its personal implications in terms of future academic options and career choices. The logic and interrelatedness of the curriculum must be made clear. Students must also be helped to grasp the significance of subject areas selected for the core curriculum.

The core curriculum is more than a random selection of topics. Students must develop a sense of how the pieces fit together – how literature, mathematics, sciences, history, the social sciences, and the arts combine to form the basis of skills, knowledge, and ideals vital to their futures.

Students must also be helped to gain a sense of curriculum continuity in relation to their studies which allows them to visualize the relationship between courses taken in grades 6, 7, and 8 and the courses they will take in high school.

The requirements of a strong academic counseling program include access by students to trusted adults who have a comprehensive grasp of the logic of the core curriculum, a broad knowledge of the academic program, and a thorough understanding of the connectedness between middle grade courses and high school curricula. It also involves the ability of teachers and counselors to communicate clearly the consequences of academic choices to students and the widening or narrowing of future options and opportunities based on personal educational decisions made in the middle grades.

A Sense of Mission

All students have a right to know why they are in school. This sounds so obvious that it seems trite to even mention it. Yet, one of the recent major national studies of American education discovered that not one student among those interviewed in more than 2,000 hours of visitations to schools could clearly and coherently express why they were there. [John Goodlad, *A Place Called School*]

Teachers and parents share the responsibility of dealing with this scandal. Unless there is a true sense of purpose, expressed in the language and concepts appropriate to each age-grade level, how can we hope to have any kind of vital, consistent commitment by students or parents or teachers to educational excellence.

If there is no clear sense of mission or commonly held sense of what the schools are doing, the results are easy to predict. There may be a blind kind of allegiance to school by the brighter children who have some kind of vague sense about loyalty to parents' and teachers' goals. But for many other students, there can be a feeling of cynicism which leads to truancy, failure and "disconnectedness."

A clear message to educators is to insist on good answers to the "what," "why," and "how" questions of each school's mission. Purposes and goals should be reviewed in practical, personal ways rather than in lofty platitudes which to young persons are nothing but words.

James, J. Fenwick, *The Middle School Years.* San Diego, Calif.: Fenwick Associates, ©1986, p. 3.

A strong academic counseling program also provides for direct, substantive parental involvement. Parents must be aware of academic opportunities, course choices, and the consequences of their children's decisions related to these matters. Parents who realize the implications of the relationship between the middle grade and secondary curricula are in a prime position to encourage and support their children's efforts to reach toward academic goals that lead to the broadest possible range of alternatives in secondary and postsecondary education.

Teachers and counselors have the most vital role to play in making certain that students have the benefits of a strong academic counseling program. There must be continuous, effective communication between teachers and counselors which ensures that the messages students receive are timely, accurate, and specific. The importance of this level of preciseness needs to be underscored. Accurate information on which to base academic plans and personal decisions about their futures is a fundamental expectation to which every middle grade student is entitled.

There are multiple reasons to justify the priority allocation of professional time to a comprehensive academic counseling program. When choices and their consequences are understood clearly, the basis for strong, positive motivation to succeed academically becomes more probable for students. Critical decisions about ninth grade courses are made in the spring of the eighth grade. Students who receive academic counseling throughout the middle grades can approach this important juncture in their education with confidence when they know that they are well prepared for their transition to high school.

A corollary of strong academic counseling is the need for assurances that students possess a level of "exit skills" and knowledge which will enable them to qualify for the broadest possible range of curriculum options at the point of high school entry. It is insufficient for students to know only about opportunities, choices, and consequences. This information must be paralleled by a close monitoring of their achievement in the core curriculum. Care must be taken to make certain that remedial, regular, or accelerated instruction pushes all students toward their maximum levels of individual ability.

In this latter context, academic counseling also means that students must develop a clear concept of their human potential. The middle grades represent critical formative years for young adolescents. It is at this point that many students form lifelong values and attitudes about the significance of education and their own chances of succeeding in upwardly mobile academic and career choices. It is for these reasons that students need to grasp conceptually the potential of their own lives. They must receive the affirmation and motivation which will cause them to strive to attain their highest and best scholastic

Academic Counseling: Reflections on the Middle Grades

The significance of [academic counseling during] the middle years is found in recognizing:

- That adolescence is a time to experience; to explore; to ask questions; to wonder; to imagine; to believe; to doubt; to feel; to sense life in its various shapes and sizes;

- That all youth need to develop unique interests; to uncover hidden talents; to experience satisfaction in accomplishments; to talk about the meaning of these things; to pursue diligently some aptitudes, abilities, and interests; to set others aside to "mellow" for awhile;

- That some youth need to press the limits of their teacher's knowledge; that the teacher's role is to provide a chart and a compass in such instances and to then step back and watch young adventurers strike out on their own for a time;

- That other youth will need extraordinary amounts of acceptance and affirmation from their teachers; that their experiences are too often threatening and destructive; that there may be no one else to whom they can turn for mature guidance and reassurance;

- That for still others, their lives are genuinely at risk; that becoming "disconnected" is a distinct possibility; that missed opportunities will not be repeated; that for whatever dreams and ambitions might be present there is no hope unless a miracle happens; that teachers and counselors have the potential to set the stage for "miracles" even if they cannot guarantee them;

- ... that all students experience deep thoughts, feelings, or events that impact indelibly the formation of their adult values; that the sensitivity and responsiveness of teachers and counselors have the potential to make enormous differences in the value systems of their students;

- That the answers to the questions "Who am I?" and "Where am I going?" are deeply imbedded in the attitudes and values that emerge in adolescence; that without positive, mature values there can be no positive, mature answers to these questions.

James J. Fenwick, *The Middle School Years.*
San Diego, Calif.: Fenwick Associates, ©1986, p. 42.

efforts. Academic counseling is a powerful factor in this process.

Equity is also a vital consideration in a strong, comprehensive academic counseling program. Every student must be touched. Every student must be challenged to succeed. Premature and superficial judgments about individual student ability and commitment must be resisted in favor of a conscious, continuous professional emphasis on human potential.

Closely paralleling this emphasis must be innovative educational policies and instructional practices which stimulate and sustain students and staff in their efforts to achieve the goals of academic counseling. The philosophical commitments inherent in academic counseling must be matched by deliberate, affirmative professional actions which permeate the entire middle grade program.

TASK FORCE RECOMMENDATIONS

① **Teachers, counselors, and principals should provide timely information and advice to students regarding the relationship between current achievement and future academic opportunities; students should be challenged to realize their highest academic potential. Steps to achieve these goals include:**

a. **Provision of information throughout grades 6, 7, and 8 regarding what knowledge and skills are required to keep open access to the broadest possible range of academic options in high school**

b. **Provision of personal counseling through-out grades 6, 7, and 8 which helps students more fully understand the specific nature of various academic options and the means by which these options can begin to be exercised as early as the middle grades**

c. **Provision of personal counseling in grade 8 which is designed to help students evaluate their choices of courses for grade 9 and to understand the ways in which these choices have the potential to impact the remainder of their high school program**

② **The State Department of Education should provide a clear definition of the recommended core curriculum scope and sequence for grades 6, 7, and 8 as a key factor in enabling teachers and counselors to help students prepare logically for the multiple academic options (curriculum paths) open to them in high school.**

Continued on next page

RECOMMENDATIONS *Continued*

❸ Teachers, counselors, and principals should provide multiple opportunities for all middle grade students to understand their human potential more fully; ways should be sought to stimulate and sustain commitment to academic and career goals through:

a. Parent-student-staff conferences

b. Group guidance activities under the co-sponsorship of middle grade and high school counselors and teachers

c. Classroom conversations with successful persons whose experiences convey identification with the value struggles and personal aspirations of young adolescents

d. Motivational assemblies which inspire and encourage commitment to positive educational values and personal ideals

e. Printed materials which show graphically the relationship between relative levels of success in the middle grades and access to the varied levels of academic options (curriculum paths) in high school and post secondary education

f. Widespread distribution, with classroom discussion, of the publication *Futures* (available from the California State Department of Education) to eighth grade students

g. Teacher based advisor-advisee programs

❹ Teachers, counselors, and principals should share responsibilities related to academic counseling. Given the disparities among districts in terms of staffing patterns, schedules, professional contracts, and

RECOMMENDATIONS *Continued*

financial resources, there should be collegial planning regarding ways to best achieve the goals of academic counseling within local district constraints.

⑤ Principals and teachers should evaluate school practices which affect academic counseling; improvements should be made where needed. Suggested benchmarks include evidence that:

a. Students can express their purposes for being in school and show awareness of the relationship between their present studies and their future academic options and potential career choices.

b. Students experience a high level of intellectual stimulation consistent with individual abilities.

c. Classrooms provide active, lively learning environments where students are challenged, excited, and motivated to push toward successively higher levels of personal academic achievement.

d. Limited-English-proficient students are intellectually challenged in ways that are free of English literacy dependency, when indicated.

e. Students deficient in basic skills, irrespective of their literacy level, are given frequent opportunities to develop higher-order thinking skills consistent with the intellectual development of young adolescents.

f. Mentors and/or tutors are assigned to selected students when professional

Continued on next page

RECOMMENDATIONS *Continued*

decisions indicate the appropriateness of this type of instructional support.

g. Bridges across administrative rules and protocols are built when the latter fail to respond adequately to the needs of individual students; serendipitous opportunities are seized to challenge and motivate students who fail to respond to conventional educational practices.

h. Creative strategies exist for identifying the hidden abilities, interests, and academic potential of all students.

8 Equal Access

Every middle grade student should have access to the most advanced levels of curricula offered during each of the middle grades; this opportunity should be facilitated through educational policies and practices which make the highest level of content mastery a valid and obtainable goal for vastly increased numbers of students.

The principle of *equal access* dictates that all students must be provided the opportunity to master the most advanced curricula offered during each of the middle grades. The realization of this goal requires new educational policies and practices which make it real and possible for vastly increased numbers of students to achieve at this level.

All students must experience educational equity as they strive to attain this goal. Students should be pushed as far and as fast as possible in the core curriculum subjects. Instructional practices which hinder the potential of students to reach the most advanced levels of the curricula and to achieve at the highest levels of which they are capable are unacceptable and mocks the concept of equal access.

Individual differences in learning ability often work against the attainment of the goal of equal access in middle grade classrooms. Research findings reported by Kenneth Tye support the validity of this concern:

... teachers in our junior high sample said that they did only a moderate amount of individualizing by varying instructional methods, grouping arrangements, activities, objectives, content, materials, and/or time spent on tasks. Large percentages of teachers said they never varied instruction in any of these ways for different students.

Teachers did have students work alone a good deal of the time. That, of course, was basically when they were doing ... the same thing. Such a practice was not surprising since teachers also said that they used almost no diagnostic tools to determine individual students' needs.[1]

Students do have different strengths. Individuals will invariably master the same skill or topic with different levels of sophistication and detail. Some will require valid, specific, often temporary instructional help that may be impossible to provide adequately within heterogeneously grouped classes. When this need occurs, however, instructional support services which

1 Kenneth Tye, *The Junior High: A School in Search of a Mission.* Lanham, Md.: University Press of America, Inc., ©1985, p. 344.

Excellence and Equity

The concepts of excellence and equity mean a variety of things to educators. Excellence speaks of curriculums with both breadth and depth, of knowledge that is most worthwhile, of intellectual skills that push at the limits of the mind, and of academic achievement that represents the cutting edge of each student's abilities. Equity speaks of justice, fairness, and impartiality in terms of access to the conditions of excellence.

While court mandates and legislative fiats have had great significance in moving the ideas of excellence and equity closer together within American education, they are not sufficient conditions in and of themselves. They continue to provide the foundations on which public educational policy must be built but the application of this policy is largely a function of those who administer schools at the grass roots level. Whether we talk of remote rural areas or vast urban districts, it is increasingly apparent that the power to achieve excellence and equity rests with those who are willing to risk against the odds community by community.

James J. Fenwick, *The Middle School Years.* San Diego, Calif.: Fenwick Associates, ©1986, p. 9.

are provided through categorical programs should be integrated within the school schedule in such a way that affected students still spend a maximum amount of time daily in their regular core curriculum classes.

When instructional help is provided to students through categorical programs, stereotypes must be avoided which directly or indirectly imply negative distinctions based on ethnicity, gender, general ability, primary language, or handicap.

Heterogeneous grouping practices should be normative in middle grade classrooms. If permanent or semipermanent "ability" grouping or tracking occurs for all or most of a student's school day, substantial harm can result. Researchers are invariably consistent in their conclusion that large numbers of poor and minority students, in particular, are precluded from realizing the true meaning of equal access when tracking occurs.

2 John I. Goodlad, *A Place Called School.* New York: McGraw Hill Book Company, ©1984, p. 156-57.

John Goodlad observes:

... Consistent with the findings of virtually every study that has considered the distribution of poor and minority students among track levels in schools, minority students were found in disproportionately large percentages in the low track classes of the multiracial schools in our sample. ...

There appear to be in our data, then, clear evidences of tracking's differentiating students in regard to their access to knowledge and, further, doing so disproportionately for minority students, especially poor minority students....[2]

When students require specialized instruction outside their regular classrooms, their entry and exit points should be fluid. No student should become locked into any instructional program because of scheduling complexities or other organizational rationalizations.

The task of individualizing instruction within heterogeneously grouped classrooms requires a deliberate departure from conventional teaching practices. One of the most promising approaches involves the organization of the core curriculum around a series of in-depth projects which allow wide latitude in terms of addressing individual learning differences. Students are assigned the same projects, but variations occur in the way they are completed. These variations involve the quantities of reading and writing required and the levels of detail expected in the application of knowledge and skills.

The urgency attached to the goal of *equal access* provides strong motivation to educators to introduce more individualized instructional practices   in   heterogeneously

A Teacher's Perspective

Of course, students with different skills are going to participate differently. If you are a student with below grade level reading, it's going to be harder for you to get the same experiences out of an experiment as someone well above grade level. You will need help in reading the science book and help in writing your observations. The teacher will have to provide direct instruction in reading and writing in the context of that science unit. But that direct instruction will be in response to an immediate need of the student to complete an assignment that is inherently, intrinsically more interesting and engaging than marching through repetitive skill sheets. So we're not saying that skills instruction is unnecessary; we are saying that the curriculum should be organized sequentially around content and the skills instruction inserted into that curriculum. Thus, rather than exaggerating differences in ability levels, which creates seemingly insurmountable instructional management problems, we will be diminishing the impact of individual differences and reducing the complexity of the teacher's management task. It changes the whole classroom management situation; heterogeneous grouping becomes practical and possible.

grouped classes. Curricula can be organized to emphasize units of study designed around content goals common to student assignments rather than around other learning outcomes which distinguish – even alienate – students from each other. This approach contrasts sharply with instructional practices that are organized around basic skills mastery and only emphasize and exaggerate student differences.

The goal of equal access takes on a totally new dimension when innovative educational practices permeate heterogeneously grouped core curriculum classes. Vastly increased numbers of students can be provided the opportunity to move in the direction of the most advanced levels of the curricula.

TASK FORCE RECOMMENDATIONS

① Local school boards should review and redefine district policies, as necessary, in order to provide explicitly for the right of every middle grade student to have the opportunity to master the highest and best curricula offered in each of the middle grades. In order to achieve this goal, local school boards are urged to adopt the following policy statement or to amend existing policies, as required, in order to provide essential guarantees to students.

Recommended policy:

All middle grade students shall have access to the core curriculum. Students eligible for instructional support services through district, state, or federal categorical programs shall receive assistance designed to help them succeed in the core curriculum; categorical funds shall not be used to support a remedial curriculum which displaces the time and attention which students are required to devote to the core subjects.

No student shall be tracked in grades 6, 7, and 8 according to ethnicity, gender, general ability, primary language, or handicap.

To the extent practicable for each subject, instruction shall be organized around knowledge central to the curriculum rather than

Continued on next page

RECOMMENDATIONS *Continued*

around a sequence of skills so that students who vary in skill level can study common areas of knowledge together.

Grouping by skill level for remedial or accelerated learning shall be defined on the basis of valid, specific instructional purposes and for stipulated periods of time.

❷ Local district curriculum specialists should assist teachers in formulating professional practices which ensure equal access, equal instruction, and equal opportunity for students as they seek to attain the highest levels of content mastery in the core curricula. These practices should:

a. Involve students in helping to structure their own learning.

b. Recognize human variability in learning.

c. Utilize a variety of classroom organizational patterns, including independent study, small-group and large-group instruction, tutorials, mentoring, and cooperative learning.

d. Utilize educational technology, when appropriate.

e. Emphasize the development of higher-order thinking skills as a correlate of both subject matter mastery and the continuing development of basic literacy and computational skills.

f. Stress mastery of multiple instructional practices which emphasize "active learning" classrooms.

g. Employ school schedules and related organizational practices which ensure maximum flexibility in allowing students requiring differentiated instruction to move easily back and forth between specialized and regular classrooms.

9   Student Diversity and Underrepresented Minorities

Every underrepresented minority middle grade student should receive encouragement and incentives to pursue academic and occupational goals.

The American sense of justice, contemporary law, and social norms combine to protect the rights of diverse racial groups, both genders, the handicapped, and the socioeconomically disadvantaged. These varied expressions of legal and moral commitments profoundly affect the socialization process and the psychological character of teacher-student interaction in the middle grades. They allow diversity among students to be honored and encourage knowledge and appreciation of differences in cultures and value systems.

One of the most critical issues posed by a culturally diverse student population is the manner in which attention is paid to individuals. Differentiation of the core curriculum on the basis of ethnic, linguistic, or other educationally superficial criteria is fundamentally wrong.   Practices which keep blacks, Hispanics, and other minorities outside the strong academic mainstream of the middle grades thwart their academic growth and severely limit their access to secondary and postsecondary education.

Middle grade students must be challenged to achieve cultural, scientific, and mathematical literacy through core curriculum studies. These studies have the potential to unlock unlimited futures for students, irrespective of ethnic and linguistic differences, handicapping conditions, gender, or socioeconomic variables.

We are alarmed, however, about our prospects for achieving this goal. The report of the California Commission on the Teaching Profession, *Who Will Teach Our Children? – A Strategy for Improving California's Schools*, indicates:

Hispanics represent about one-fourth of the state's K–12 population but only about one-tenth of the students in The California State University (CSU) system. ... only 4.9 percent of Hispanic high school graduates and 3.6 percent of black high school graduates are academically eligible for admission to the University of California. For The California State University, the comparable figures are 15.3 percent and 10.1 percent, respectively.[1]

It is in the middle grades that new and heroic efforts must be made to shape the hopes, aspirations, and educational goals of underrepresented minorities. A study by The California State University calls for an outreach by college and university personnel to Hispanic students in grades six through nine. This is seen as absolutely essential for a substantial improvement in the college-going rate of this group:

... significant numbers of Hispanic students do not take appropriate courses during these critical years to develop the necessary skills to undertake college preparatory study in high school.[2]

As a result of the *Final Report of the Commission on Hispanic*

1 *Who Will Teach Our Chidren? A Strategy for Improving California's Schools.* Sacramento: The California Commission on the Teaching Profession, 1985, p. 40.

2 *Hispanics and Higher Education: A CSU Imperative – Final Report of the Commission on Hispanic Underrepresentation.* Long Beach, Calif.: Office of the Chancellor, The California State University, 1985, p. vii.

Underrepresentation, The California State University and the California State Department of Education successfully gained the support of the California Legislature for a collaborative program in selected intermediate schools beginning in January, 1987. This effort deserves the careful attention of all middle grade educators.

The *Secondary School Program Quality Criteria*, published in 1985 by the California State Department of Education, stresses the urgency of helping students gain an extended educational perspective. This

3 *Secondary School Program Quality Criteria.* Sacramento: California State Department of Education, ©1985, p. 19.

goal is of special significance for underrepresented minority students:

Parents, teachers, and counselors help students set a path that aims toward their highest, most realistic goals. Students are able to discuss their program of studies, life goals, and career ambitions with their teachers and counselors. A schoolwide system of guidance facilitates such interaction and emphasizes the collaborative nature of the processes of course selection. ...

Students are encouraged to develop a four-year perspective and to clarify their goals accordingly. They understand and experience how what they are learning is interrelated. They feel that what they are learning is important to their lives now and in the future.[3]

In order for these goals to be realized, it is urgent that English be taught more efficiently and effectively to California's large and growing population of limited-English-proficient students. These youths are too often relegated to a barren curriculum of remedial skills that does not prepare them for high school coursework in literature, science, history, or mathematics. They are effectively foreclosed from any realistic considerations of higher education goals.

The middle grades represent the critical juncture. New ways must be found to interest, excite, challenge, and reward young adolescents who are from underrepresented minorities. They must be helped to focus their attention on positive academic values and their corollaries of higher education and upwardly mobile careers.

The educational challenge posed by differences in cultures and value

Scholarship Pledges

A new idea is abroad in the country. It seems to have begun in New York when businessman Eugene M. Lang spontaneously promised a class of 51 Harlem sixth-graders that, if they finished high school, he would give each of them a $2,000 college scholarship and add to it each year they remained in school. That was in 1981. Lang says he now expects 50 of those students to graduate from high school.

Since then, at least 19 other cities have expressed an interest in starting similar programs, according to a recent article in *Education Week.*

In Dallas, the STEP Foundation has been organized and has gathered enough pledges from businesses and community groups to provide college scholarships for 1,000 students now in the sixth grade.

In Boston, an even more ambitious program is under way. Business leaders recently announced a plan to create a $6 million endowment that would guarantee scholarship help for every high school graduate who needs it. Money from the endowment will also be used to hire high school counselors to assist students in obtaining other financial aid.

This is not to suggest that local businesses have not contributed to the public schools. Many participate in adopt-a-school programs or have contributed to other school projects. But so far California has not produced the kind of broad support for students that is envisioned in other states. Perhaps it's time to consider it. What a wonderful way it would be for the businesses that benefit from being in the community to help provide for its future well-being.

systems is summarized in the recent Carnegie Report, *A Nation Prepared: Teachers for the 21st Century:*

Yet another factor has widespread educational implications: growing numbers of disadvantaged students — from low-income families, non-English-speaking backgrounds, and single-parent households. All youngsters need teachers with a much more sophisticated and complete understanding of their subjects, but the need of these children is greatest. These children, many of them the product of generations of poverty, find little in their environment outside of school that matches the affluent youngsters' push for academic success and the belief that it will pay off.[4]

Businesses, industries, the professions, and colleges and universities must help in this task. There are many exciting examples of where this is now happening. Thousands of other students need the same level of personal attention.

The California State University, the University of California, and private universities and colleges should make long-range financial aid commitments to underrepresented minority students as early as the middle grades, contingent on solid academic achievement throughout high school.

The need for public school teachers drawn from the ranks of underrepresented minorities is especially acute. Again, the Carnegie Report pinpoints the urgency of this need:

Leaving aside for the moment the need to improve school performance greatly, the demographic realities just described alone pose an impressive problem for education policymakers.

Taken together, a steep increase in demand for teachers, a particularly acute need for minority teachers, and a declining supply of well-educated applicants constitute a challenge without precedent — an environment very different from the one in which the advances of the last three years have been made.[5]

The situation described by the Carnegie Report reflects particularly acute needs in California. The state's "public schools will soon be 43 percent minority; by the year 2000 that figure will be more than 50 percent."[6] Our schools must be staffed by teachers who reflect the diversity of the state's racial and cultural heritage. This means that we must do a dramatically better job of ensuring that underrepresented minority students in the middle grades are prepared academically for high school and subsequent entry into institutions of higher learning. A vastly increased pool of candidates must become available to consider teaching as well as other professions which require higher education as a prerequisite for entry.

The identification of potential minority teachers should occur as early as the middle grades and should be accompanied by intensive mentoring primarily provided by members of the teaching profession. Mentors should be recruited from the public schools and from the ranks of college and university professors, as well as from business and industry.

The state Legislature should provide scholarship funds for minority individuals who choose to enter the teaching profession and who main-

4 *A Nation Prepared: Teachers for the 21st Century.* Washington, D.C.: Carnegie Forum on Education and the Economy, ©1986, p. 32. This report was prepared by the Carnegie Forum on Education and the Economy's Task Force on Teaching as a Profession. The Carnegie Forum is a program of the Carnegie Corporation of New York.

5 Ibid.

6 *Education USA*, Vol. 28 (May 5, 1986), p. 281, ©1986. Reprinted by permission from *Education USA*, National School Public Relations Association.

tain their academic standing to the point of certification.

It is a charade to laud student diversity as a reflection of the richness of our cultural heritage when multitudes of underrepresented minority students fall far short of realizing their intellectual and occupational potential. It is imperative to reverse this situation. Public schools and institutions of higher education must take the lead in attaining this goal.

TASK FORCE RECOMMENDATIONS

❶ Local school boards and superintendents should review and redefine middle grade policies and administrative regulations in order to deliberately and affirmatively expose minority students to a strong academic mainstream leading to higher education and the professions. Districts are encouraged to:

a. **Establish successively higher annual targets leading to substantive increases in the percentages of minority middle grade students who are prepared for and actually enroll in high school courses which meet college and university admissions requirements.**

b. **Establish a program at each middle grade school with a significant underrepresented minority enrollment which provides students with extra help in mastering knowledge and skills needed to succeed in a college preparatory curriculum. This help should include:**

- **Study skills techniques**
- **Learning to learn strategies**

Continued on next page

RECOMMENDATIONS *Continued*

- Communication skills (particularly those which emphasize written and spoken expression)
- Test-taking skills
- Academic counseling
- Problem-solving strategies in mathematics

c. Utilize instructional materials which honor individual and group diversity and which portray positive images and high expectations for students in a multicultural society.

d. Ensure that students with limited literacy, irrespective of whether or not English is their native language, are allowed to enroll in regular core curriculum courses which emphasize the development of higher-order thinking skills.

❷ The State Department of Education, independent research institutions, and local districts with research and evaluation units should develop new measures of academic potential to identify students whose intellectual promise is obscured by linguistic barriers or other factors which cause them to do poorly on standardized tests.

❸ Public and private colleges and universities, businesses, industries, and the professions should assist school districts in developing tutorial and mentoring programs which reach underrepresented minority students on a one-to-one basis; tutors and mentors should provide instruction, affirmation, and motivation to students designed to bring about a significant expansion of the numbers of underrepresented minorities who enroll in institutions of higher education and who enter upwardly mobile career fields.

Continued on next page

RECOMMENDATIONS *Continued*

④ The California State University, the University of California, and private colleges and universities should identify (and ultimately support through varied financial assistance programs) underrepresented minority students beginning in the middle grades; they should plan programs which encourage the ultimate enrollment of these students in institutions of higher education.

⑤ The California Legislature should authorize and fund a teacher recruitment program directed to underrepresented minorities. Identification of students with potential interest in becoming teachers should begin as early as the middle grades. Higher education scholarships should be provided for underrepresented minority students who successfully complete professional teacher preparation programs.

10 At-Risk Students

Many middle grade students are "at risk" of dropping out of school; they should have access to educational programs which emphasize personal commitments to academic achievement.

The term "at risk" has emerged in the American press as a shorthand expression for students who, although still in school, are up for grabs. For whatever reason these students are not connected with the purposes of the school. They have not identified sufficiently with its values and are at risk of becoming dropouts.

The search for independence and autonomy annually leads a frightening number of youths to disengage from home and school by the end of the middle grade years or soon thereafter. Findings reported by the National Center for Educational Statistics (NCES) indicate that 700,000 adolescents leave school each year prior to high school graduation. These students move beyond the sphere of influence which provides the majority of young adolescents with some measure of stability and security. The Education Commission of the States refers to such students as "disconnected youth." The urgency of addressing the needs of these students lies in salvaging their lives not only for moral, ethical, and intellectual reasons, but also for the sake of the nation's economic and social well-being.

Gene Maeroff, education writer for *The New York Times,* puts it well when he says:

A solution must be found because the issue "raises the question of how long a democractic society can continue to exist" when the nation is producing thousands and thousands of people who are unable to function in that society.[1]

Early adolescence represents the most critical period in the education of students. Although at risk, most of the identifiable potential dropouts are still in school during the middle grades. There is still hope for them.

1 *Education USA,* Vol. 27. (July 22, 1985), p. 347, ©1985. Reprinted by permission from *Education USA,* National School Public Relations Association.

The Economics of Dropping-Out

The cost of dropping out of school should become required reading for every middle grade student. Those who can't read should have the data read to them. Recently reported figures indicate that males, on the average, who finish high school will have lifetime earnings of $266,000 more than those who drop out (Professor James S. Catterall, UCLA Graduate School of Education). The comparable figure for females is $199,000.

The net cost to both individuals and their communities is staggering. It has been estimated that the economic loss attributable to the dropouts in a single school class of a major city such as Los Angeles, Chicago, or New York will aggregate more than three *billion* dollars.

It is sometimes argued, and perfectly true, that the dollars aren't important, that the human cost is what really counts. But dollars, in this case, are a relevant measure of the human cost, and one which illustrates the magnitude of the difficulty.

Someone should sit down with all potentially at-risk students and say: "Look I know school is hard and that you don't like it very well, that it gets in the way of other things that seem more exciting, that you don't think you're learning anything worthwhile. You can walk away from it all – but if you choose to do that, it'll cost you about a quarter of a million dollars. The price is very steep and you may not realize what you're giving up."

Most potential dropouts may reasonably say "I never thought I'd see that kind of money in my whole life." The answer is: "Right! And if you drop out the chances are you never will!"

In practical terms, large numbers of other middle grade students are also at risk. Early adolescence is a volatile time. Intense physical, psychological, social, and intellectual changes mean that few students escape unscathed.

Organizational and instructional priorities of sound middle grade education programs have particular meaning for at-risk students. For example, provision of extended blocks of instructional time for selected core curriculum subjects has the potential to allow every student to be known personally by one or more teachers. This arrangement also gives teachers and counselors an opportunity to monitor systematically the progress of each student. When learning difficulties occur, those who best know the student are in a position to pool their observations and recommendations and to develop strategies for coping with particular needs.

Extended blocks of instructional time also make it possible for students to experience identification and friendship with peers. Cooperative learning strategies in particular reinforce positive peer group values and commitment to educational goals.

The use of tutors and mentors can be particularly helpful in working with at-risk students. The power of these two types of support systems is extensively documented in educational research literature. Each has the potential to provide simple yet strategic one-to-one levels of interaction. These can address a wide range of needs ranging from the remediation of basic skills to the development of deep friendships, with mutually positive educational consequences for all students involved.

At-risk students are typically deficient in basic skills. They may be assigned to extensive blocks of remedial instruction. This remediation often backfires because it reinforces negative self-perceptions by emphasizing the students past failures. Remedial exercises may represent the very kind of abstract, meaningless activity which at-risk students find most difficult to accept. By way of contrast, these students can often learn best by working on specific, concrete assignments involving basic skills which have a direct relationship to the "real world" which they are

Academic Success and Educational Commitment

Every student needs success experiences. Students identified as at-risk rarely experience either success or affirmation. Most are compelled to conform to instructional situations which have a built-in failure quotient. Success is dependent upon the very qualities which students most lack. For those who are literate, who have the ability to succeed but don't, we should recognize the compelling research which identifies massive boredom as one of the primary causes for dropping out of school. Instructional practices should be varied and responsive to the needs of students for success and challenge.

Teachers, counselors, and principals should reaffirm continuously their professional commitment to the basic mission of the middle grades: to create the conditions for academic success and educational commitment for every student. Professionals who work in the middle grades must believe that adolescence is a time to be celebrated intellectually and emotionally. The modeled behavior which students see daily in their teachers represents the single most vital factor in shaping personal commitments and educational values.

experiencing during early adolescence.

Students who have even the most acute deficiencies in basic skills need to experience the intellectual excitement of higher-order thought processes. Instructional time devoted to basic skills deficiencies should never preempt the opportunity of students to explore the cutting edges of thoughts and feelings embedded in the subject matter of the core curriculum. These include the intellectual and emotional experiences found in great literature, history, science, mathematics, and the arts.

Ethnic identity and status are also critical variables in the lives of many at-risk students. Cultural support systems are an urgent requirement in many instances, particularly among limited-English-proficient students. It is important for these young adolescents to feel and know the inherent power and beauty of their own language.

Non-English-speaking students who are in transition from their native language to English temporarily sacrifice the most fundamental dimension of their own culture. Language patterns shape thought in profound ways. Shifting to a radically different grammar, syntax, vocabulary, and idiomatic base can be a painful and difficult experience.

Large numbers of limited-English-proficient students feel a sense of despair that permeates their academic goals and educational values. Many retreat into the relative security of their native language

without crossing the threshold of English fluency. Teachers and counselors who understand this phenomenon in terms of its psychological impact are in a position to help many at-risk students succeed.

"At Risk" Students and the Lesson of the Peer Group

... Adolescence is a precarious time when little in the lives of students may appear to be worthy of praise. Yet they long to be valued as individuals. William James, recognized as the most eminent American psychologist of this century, has said that "the need to be appreciated represents the most profound desire of the human heart." Teachers must ask themselves, "Am I an affirmer or an infirmer?" There is no other single technique which is more powerful in breaking down the generational walls than for adolescents to find adults who affirm them as persons. To have another individual express belief in you as a worthy human being in spite of your acne, awkwardness, and inexperience can be overwhelming.

It is the "affirmation principle" which is at work in the adolescent's allegiance to the peer group. "I'm OK-you're OK." It is equally the same phenomenon that produces rock star heroes whose influences sweep through the lives of millions of youth. A study of the lyrics of musical hits leaves no doubt that the individuals who write, sing, and play them not only know how to tune in on the emotional wave lengths of adolescents; they also know how to affirm them as human beings with significant thoughts and feelings. Is it any wonder that those who hold these keys to the emotions and intellects turn into modern day pied pipers – and millionaires?

For teachers, counselors, and principals the challenge is to build bridges rather than to string barbed wire between themselves and students. No one does the latter either deliberately or capriciously. We do it without knowing the measure of our words or actions. The lesson of the peer group is "affirmation." This principle is powerful; it may represent the single most effective, cost-efficient deterrent to adult-student alienation available. Moreover, it can be put into effect immediately by almost anyone with rapid and observable consequences. A faculty dedicated to the "principle of affirmation" can significantly reduce the distance between adult values and peer group norms. When this principle is systematically implemented, an entire student body can be turned around.

James J. Fenwick, *The Middle School Years*, San Diego, Calif.: Fenwick Associates, ©1986, p. 82.

Transiency represents another major cause of instability. High levels of mobility take a particularly heavy toll on young adolescents. California schools currently serve over 125,000 migrant students whose academic vulnerability is staggering. But migrants are not alone. Transiency rates in the general population are high and cut through all socioeconomic levels.

Poor communication among schools – even within the same district – can create a critical lag time that works to the disadvantage of students and may result in further separation and alienation for those whose relationship to school is already tenuous. Computerized student information networks represent one answer to this dilemma. These networks need to become more common. They have the potential to allow direct school-to-school transmission of student record facsimiles and to enable personalized teacher-to-teacher communication to occur, when appropriate.

For many students, the middle grades may represent their last substantive educational experience. As noted earlier, the dropout statistics accelerate rapidly during the early years of high school. A solid philosophy of middle grade education can blunt these statistics and move large numbers of at-risk or potentially at-risk students into the future with a spirit of courage and hope.

TASK FORCE RECOMMENDATIONS

➊ Local school boards should mandate at least one extended time block daily in two or more of the core curriculum subjects during the middle grades to ensure that:

   a. Every middle grade student is known personally and well by one or more teachers.

   b. Individual monitoring of student progress takes place systematically so that teachers and counselors can quickly identify learning difficulties and take corrective measures.

   c. Cooperative learning strategies are implemented as a means of building strong positive peer group relationships and reinforcing essential educational values and goals.

➋ Superintendents should give leadership in helping principals devise means for reducing the pressure of large complex schools which leaves many students with a sense of anonymity and isolation. Particular attention should be given to organizational and scheduling concepts which are student-centered and which maximize opportunities for strong personal bonds among smaller numbers of students and teachers throughout the full span of the middle grade years.

➌ Local school boards should authorize and fund peer, cross-age, and/or adult tutorial and mentor programs in the middle grades as a proven response to the needs of many at-risk students.

Continued on next page

RECOMMENDATIONS *Continued*

④ The State Department of Education and local district curriculum departments should assist teachers in devising instructional strategies that allow students with basic skills deficiencies to engage in learning experiences which develop higher-order thinking skills; these strategies should correspond with core curriculum goals and should enable students to learn in regular classrooms; and learning experiences should be consistent with the maturity and interest levels of young adolescents.

⑤ Principals should give leadership in creating cultural support systems for students – particularly those with limited-English-proficiency – whose self identity is threatened through the loss and implicit devaluing of their native language; teachers and counselors should understand the psychological trauma involved in the transition from one language to another and the bearing which this phenomenon has on the negative attitudes and values of some categories of at-risk students.

⑥ Teachers, counselors, and principals should continuously model behavior which affirms their commitment to the basic mission of those who work in the middle grades: to enjoy young adolescents and to create conditions for academic success and educational commitment for every student.

11 Physical and Emotional Development

Many middle grade students require specific primary health care services and strong counseling and guidance programs in order to be able to concentrate their intellectual abilities on academic goals.

There is a direct, intrinsic relationship between intellectual development and physical and emotional health. The fundamental role of student support services is to address the physical and emotional health needs of students in order to further the development of their minds and to enhance the potential for the realization of their academic goals:

Psychologists tell us that the traumas of the adolescent years tend not to be taken too seriously by adults – teachers included. Failure to do so lies at the root of some of the most serious interpersonal conflicts in the middle grades – conflicts that involve fractured relationships among both students and teachers. These may have crippling, even tragic consequences. While violence, per se, is the exception, the damage to personality development through warped values and academic failure have the potential ultimately to exact a bitter price from the individual and from society.

The transition to adolescence represents a genuine period of danger physically and emotionally for youth. Accidental death, suicide, drug abuse, and crime are statistically disproportionate during the teen years. Psychologists observe that normal, healthy adolescents are, by adult standards, variously manic, depressed, and even psychopathic in their behaviors as they confront turbulent, shifting, and often conflicting emotions and events in their lives. It is unconscionable professionally to ignore these facts. One cannot pretend that educational excellence can be achieved in an academic setting that dismisses the impact of adolescent traumas as little more than emotional trivia to be tolerated until they somehow go away.[1]

Middle grade education draws much of its special character from deliberate attempts to admit and respond to the tension which exists between the goals of academic achievement and the personal developmental needs of young adolescents. In a study of 130 "exemplary" middle schools, reported by the Association for Supervision and Curriculum Development (ASCD), the authors conclude:

"... one of the long-espoused goals of the middle school has been to focus on the unique nature and needs of young adolescents. Our results indicate that exemplary middle schools have been very successful in promoting student personal development."[2]

This same study reports positive outcomes related to the successful implementation of a middle grade educational philosophy which considers intellectual, physical, and emotional issues as complementary variables:

... Over 80 percent of the respondents testified that student emotional health, creativity, and confidence in self-directed learning were positively affected.... Over 90 percent believed that student self-concept and social development also benefited.

Not a single respondent reported negative effects on student personal development. The success of team organization and teacher-based guidance in helping individuals develop closer peer relationships was cited repeatedly. Extracurricular and intramural athletic activities were open to all students and invited greater student participation, interaction, and competition. Awards for leadership, good

1 James J. Fenwick, *The Middle School Years.* San Diego, Calif.: Fenwick Associates, ©1986, p. 28.

2 Paul S. George and Lynn L. Oldaker, "A National Survey of Middle School Effectiveness," *Educational Leadership*, Vol. 42. (December, 1985/January, 1986), p. 80. Reprinted with permission of the Association for Supervision and Curriculum Development. ©1986 by the Association for Supervision and Curriculum Development. All rights reserved.

citizenship, and cooperation in and out of classes enabled those who weren't honor roll students or star athletes to experience the important satisfaction of peer recognition. Interdisciplinary teams, classroom guidance, and exploratory programs increased opportunities for student involvement and accomplishments, significantly improving student personal development.[3]

Lipsitz's findings support these same conclusions:

A central weakness in most schools for young adolescents is a widespread failure to reconsider each school practice in terms of developmental needs in order either to incorporate responsibility for meeting them into the schools' academic and social goals or to keep them from being barriers to attaining those goals. ... Decisions about governance, curriculum, and school organization, while different in each school, flow from this sensitivity to the age group. Given massive individual differences in development during early adolescence, it is doubtful that a school for the age group could be successful without this sensitivity.[4]

The most striking feature of the ... schools is their willingness and ability to adapt all school practices to the individual differences in intellectual, biological, and social maturation of their students. The schools take seriously what is known about early adolescent development, especially its interindividual and intraindividual variability. This seriousness is reflected in decisions they make about all aspects of school life.[5]

Lipsitz underscores her conclusions by observing that the schools in her research set out to be positive environments for early adolescent personal and social development, not only because such environments contribute to academic achievement but also because they are intrinsically valued.

Substantial evidence indicates the compromised physical health of adolescents. A recent report from the President's Council on Physical Fitness and Sports indicates that many early adolescents are badly out of shape, in spite of the national fitness craze. George Allen, chairman of the Council, states, *"The best-kept secret in the United States today is youth fitness, or lack of it. Kids have no endurance, no strength, and very little flexibility."*

Major causes of death in this country are diseases of the heart and blood vessels, problems with a known link to a sedentary lifestyle. A 1983 study of 1500 Los Angeles fourth-graders, examined by a UCLA research group, showed that nearly one-half of these students exhibited at least one major risk factor associated with heart disease, arteriosclerosis, and stroke. These risk factors included high blood pressure, high cholesterol, and obesity.[6]

Young adolescents must learn more about the significance of personal health and fitness. They should understand the relationship between a healthy lifestyle and intellectual and emotional development. They should learn to make positive health decisions that reduce the risk of chronic diseases. Middle grade educators must address these concerns. Efforts should concentrate on health practices which relate to proper nutrition; cardiovascular fitness; the development of flexibility, stamina, and physical strength; and avoidance of experimentation with mind-altering drugs and

3 Ibid., pp. 80-81.

4 Published by permission of Transaction, Inc., from *Successful Schools for Young Adolescents,* by Joan Lipsitz, ©1984 by Transaction, Inc., p. 168.

5 Ibid., p. 167.

6 *The Los Angeles Times.* (May 9, 1986).

Physical and Emotional Development 73

inhalants. The latter concern is dramatized by the findings of a statewide survey involving over 7000 California students (see box), indicating a major surge in drug use occurring between the seventh and ninth grades!

The importance of emotional health as a primary goal of middle grade education must be equally affirmed. Although emotional health is fostered in many ways, its primary focus should be in the classroom. Mergendoller and Marchman provide a powerful and succinct discussion of several of the major issues involved:

If this [facilitating students' psychological health] *is considered a worthwhile goal for educators, it is important to consider the norms characterizing individual classrooms and reflect on how norms appropriate for constructive peer interaction can be established. As teachers reprimand students for inappropriate behavior and reward them for proper conduct, they help to establish norms for classroom deportment.*

We do not espouse a universal list of norms that teachers should establish in order to facilitate a constructive social climate, as we believe it is best left up to individual instructors to establish expectations appropriate for their subjects, schools, and students. At a minimum, however, we would expect that teachers should model respectful social relationships. Students, like everyone else, are more often influenced by example than by exhortation. In addition, teachers can contribute to the establishment of positive social climates by prohibiting putdowns and other negative forms of interaction. Note that this does not mean that a teacher must accept all answers as correct in class discussion, ignore the distinction between effort and accomplishment, apologize for

knowing more than students, or otherwise distort the distinctions that make the relationship between teacher and student different than the relationships students have with their peers. A peer, as we noted earlier, is an equal, and in classrooms teachers are more than equal. They must maintain positions of legitimate, expert

Alcohol, Drug, and Inhalant Use Among California's Adolescent Population

A statewide survey has found that more than half of California's high school juniors have experimented with drugs and 85% have tried alcohol, with the highest use reported in rural areas and among white students.

The survey, called the first of its kind in California, found that a major surge in drug use occurs between the seventh and ninth grades. By the 11th grade, the study discovered, more students are smoking marijuana than tobacco cigarettes.

"It is a sad and sobering reality that trying drugs is no longer the exception among high school students," said Attorney General John Van de Kamp, who commissioned the study. "It is the norm."

"Surprisingly," Van de Kamp told a press conference," the survey found proportionately higher drug and alcohol use among junior high and high school students in rural areas of California than in Los Angeles and other cities."

The survey of 7,379 students in the seventh, ninth, and eleventh grades was conducted by Rodney Skager, Associate Dean of the UCLA Graduate School of Education. Skager said the students were selected at random from 87 secondary schools around the state and guaranteed anonymity.

According to the survey, 10.7% of the seventh graders reported using illegal drugs at least once. Nearly 58% said they had tried alcohol, but only 15.8% said they had actually gotten drunk.

Among the ninth graders, 35.7% said they had tried drugs, while 77.6% said they had tried alcohol and 47.1% said they had become intoxicated.

Marijuana was by far the most commonly used drug, followed by cocaine, amphetamines, and inhalants such as glue. Among seventh graders, however, inhalants were the most commonly used drug.

Because of the increase in drug, inhalant, and alcohol use between seventh and ninth grades, Van de Kamp called for educational prevention programs to begin as early as kindergarten.

Rodney Skager, Dennis Fisher, and Ebrahim Maddahien, *A Statewide Survey of Drug and Alcohol Use Among California Students in Grades 7, 9, and 11.* Sacramento: Office of the Attorney General, Crime Prevention Center. May, 1986.

authority if they are to have a constructive influence on students. We advocate that students are given the respect they deserve, mistakes be corrected in a businesslike manner that focuses on the error committed rather than the abilities of the person who made that error, and help be available for all students who seek it.[7]

Teachers and other professional personnel should work together in collaborative ways to ensure that the classroom emerges as the most basic setting in the school within which both psychological and physical health are stressed. In order for this type of professional collaboration to occur, specialized support personnel and services are essential:

- Students need access to on-site professionally trained counselors. Ideally, students should remain with the same counselor throughout their middle grade years.

- The professional expertise of student study teams provides a vital link among students, parents, and teachers. These teams are typically composed of members of the counseling and administrative staffs, an educational psychologist, and a school nurse. They have published guidelines and procedures for their work and meet on a regular basis to review individual student profiles, give professional guidance, and otherwise ensure collaboration in addressing specific student needs. Teachers should be frequent participants in the work of student study teams and should be released from classroom responsibilies, when necessary, in order to make participation possible.

- Attendance outreach programs represent an effective means for identifying students whose academic progress is being harmed because of poor attendance and tardiness. Outreach counselors have the ability to move freely within the community and to give valuable guidance to parents and school personnel relative to the needs of specific students.

- Students require scheduled access to school-related health support services. These services provide the basis for instruction in general health

7 John Mergendoller and Virginia Marchman, "Friends and Associates," in *Educators Handbook: Research into Practice.* White Plains, N.Y.: Longman, Inc., ©1987, p. 307.

School Clinics

The steady growth in school-based health clinics signals a recognition that traditional medical delivery systems are not reaching many adolescents, especially those in low-income communities.

Clinics do more than provide comprehensive health care. They are committed to resolving other problems of teenagers. Patient follow-up after an initial visit often means helping a teen work through academic problems, relationships with peers, or problems at home.

Clinics provide exams for athletic participation, weight control plans, nutrition information -- and some even offer a quiet place to study. All give one-on-one attention to teenagers.

In most instances so far, schools have provided in-kind services, such as space and clerical help. Funding for school clinics has come from medical schools, health agencies, Medicaid and foundations, and often a combination of these sources.

While most of the clinics are in inner cities, some are being planned for rural high schools, in conjunction with community health centers.

practices, safety, and first aid. They enable early identification of communicable diseases and offer dental, vision, and hearing screening. Medical practitioners should work closely with students, parents, and faculty in the provision of health support services. The detection and referral of cases involving child abuse, substance abuse, suicidal tendencies, pregnancy, obesity, malnourishment, and other potentially life-threatening situations represent central elements of a comprehensive program of health support services.

Preoccupation with the physical and emotional health needs of students is a direct corollary of efforts to ensure high academic standards. The complexity of early adolescence demands schools which in Lipsitz's words demonstrate *"their willingness and ability to adapt all school practices to the individual differences in intellectual, biological, and social maturation of their students."*[8]

8 Published by permission of Transaction, Inc., from *Successful Schools for Young Adolescents*, by Joan Lipsitz, ©1984 by Transaction, Inc., p. 167.

TASK FORCE RECOMMENDATIONS

① The state Legislature, with the support of the Governor and the Superintendent of Public Instruction, should authorize funds to enable scheduled access by middle grade students to school-related health services.

② Local school boards should adopt policies which provide health services in the following areas:

a. Identification and appropriate professional referral of cases involving alcohol and drug abuse, substance abuse, suicidal tendencies, pregnancies, obesity, and other types of potentially life-threatening situations

b. Cardiovascular fitness

c. Early detection of communicable diseases

d. Nutrition

e. Dental, vision, and hearing screening

Continued on next page

RECOMMENDATION *Continued*

③ The state Legislature, with the support of the Governor and the Superintendent of Public Instruction, should provide funds for middle grade schools to establish, sustain, and/or expand advising and/or counseling programs; these programs should be designed to assure students timely access to professionals who are knowledgeable about educational issues and who are sympathetic and responsive to the physical and emotional developmental needs of young adolescents. Appropriate advising and /or counseling functions include:

a. Teacher-based adviser-advisee programs which involve the same teachers and students throughout the middle grade years

b. Group guidance programs which bring students, teachers, and counselors together in shared activities designed to develop positive academic values and educational goals

c. Peer advising programs which involve mentoring relationships among students of the same or different ages

d. Conventional counseling and guidance programs with realistic professional to student ratios

④ Superintendents should authorize the formation of student study teams in schools which serve the middle grades. Team members should come primarily from among professionals already on the school staff.

Continued on next page

RECOMMENDATION *Continued*

⑤ Principals should make provisions to release teachers temporarily from their regular classroom duties in order to allow them to participate in the work of student study teams, when appropriate. Local school boards should provide funds for other support staff (e.g., nurses and psychologists) who need to be made available to student study teams on a more limited basis.

⑥ The state Legislature should authorize funds for attendance outreach programs for the middle grades which provide a professional to student ratio of 1:1500.

⑦ Local school boards, as necessary, should review and strengthen policies which facilitate cooperation with other districts and with community agencies, organizations, and institutions that provide physical and emotional support services for adolescents.

⑧ Administrators, teachers, and counselors should provide leadership in promoting interdistrict and interagency collaborative planning related to physical and emotional health support services for adolescents.

⑨ Local school boards and community agencies should work together to develop early intervention strategies for at-risk students. More stringent civil codes should be adopted in order to give such agencies as the School Attendance Review Board (SARB) greater effectiveness in the enforcement of its actions.

PART THREE

ORGANIZATION AND STRUCTURE:
Creating New Learning Environments

12 School Culture

Every middle grade student should experience a positive school culture which reflects a strong, student-centered educational philosophy.

The concept of school culture relates to the quality of the school environment which students experience daily. Quality translates into the relative excellence of curricular offerings and instructional practices. It also includes the degree to which students have the opportunity for their personalities and abilities to unfold under the sensitive care of individuals whose commitment evidences the highest levels of professional-client relationships. However one describes it, the best available evidence shows that where teachers and students experience a given constellation of positive, mutually rewarding behaviors, achievement increases significantly.

Research published by the American Association of School Administrators (AASA) analyzed school culture, among other variables, in schools previously determined as exemplary in competition sponsored by the U. S. Department of Education.[1] The findings indicate that these schools:

- Convey a sense of *order and purpose,* no matter where they were located or what their resources. The latter factors were overriden by a "a principal and a group of teachers truly dedicated to making a difference in the lives of their students."

- Provide classrooms *organized for efficiency,* with time

viewed as a "precious commodity." Similarly, assessment is systematic and objective but also continual, with results used immediately to help students.

- Exhibit *student centeredness.* This translates into a high level of interaction between students and teachers. Individual student needs figure into planning. In addition, while academics are primary, nonacademic extracurricular activities are important. The researchers stress that "limiting or abolishing participation in ... various ... after-school groups in order to free up time for academic learning indeed detracts from the unified school culture and would eliminate some unique learning opportunities. ..."

- Share *an attitude of optimism and high expectations* among both students and teachers. Teachers like adolescents.

- Show *organizational health.* Leadership is in evidence. Schools are being "led," not merely managed. The principals see themselves as instructional leaders. The organization is committed to professional growth of the staff; teachers welcome systematic efforts to evaluate

1 John E. Roueche, and George A. Baker, III, *Profiling Excellence in America's Schools.* Arlington, Vir.: American Association of School Administrators, ©1986, pp. 24-34.

their work. There is also a high level of awareness and acceptance by these schools of their communities, including high levels of parent-initiated involvement and student/staff participation in community projects.

These research findings tell us something vital about the ideals for which we should be striving in the middle grades. The school environment is a critical factor. Terms such as "ethos," "ambiance," "climate," "culture," and "the way we do things around here" describe subtle but nevertheless definable realities that have the potential to affect student attitudes significantly about themselves, their educational values, and their academic achievement.

These observations are further supported by the nationwide study of 130 outstanding middle schools reported by the Association for Supervision and Curriculum Development (ASCD). Researchers drew these conclusions about the significance of school culture:

Recent studies analyzing school effectiveness correlate learning climate with student behavior and achievement. Students who feel valued by teachers and view school as more than just a place to meet friends tend to show respect for their schools. The exemplary schools in this study developed programs that demonstrate persistent caring for students as young people and created a school environment to meet their special academic and personal needs. Predictably, respondents reported stronger school spirit since reorganization. Over 95 percent declared that students' attitudes toward school and feelings
about teachers became moderately or strongly positive. Eighty-six percent witnessed greater student participation in special interest activities, while 75 percent noted better school attendance. Descriptions of student enthusiasm for involvement in school programs ran nearly five to one in favor of changes brought about by a move to middle school organization.[2]

A strong student-centered educational philosophy is entirely compatible with high academic expectations. This type of philosophy is a hallmark of excellence in schools which serve the middle grades. It is important to affirm the conviction that education in the middle grades should take place in a setting specifically designed to meet the academic, personal, and social needs and goals of students. Responding to the intensity of this challenge, while maintaining a clear perspective about the fundamental academic mission of public schooling, requires a strong hand on the helm in schools which serve young adolescents.

2 Paul S. George and Lynn L. Oldaker, "A National Survey of Middle School Effectiveness," *Educational Leadership*, Vol. 42. (December, 1985/January, 1986), p. 81. Reprinted with permission of the Association for Supervision and Curriculum Development. ©1986 by the Association for Supervision and Curriculum Development. All rights reserved.

Cause and Effect

There is no simple cause-and-effect model to account for successful schools for young adolescents. Explanations seem circular. For instance, stable student attendance is a prerequisite for success in learning; success in learning leads to high attendance rates. Dedicated teachers are essential in school performance; good schools attract dedicated teachers. Community support appears to improve school outcomes; student discipline and achievement result in community support for schools. The components of successful schools, like the components of failing schools, are inextricably interrelated. ... schools ... cannot establish this complex pattern of positive interrelationships without making a serious commitment to developmental responsiveness. The attainment of each characteristic of successful schools is dependent on recognizing and working with pressing aspects of growth and development during early adolescence.

Published by permission of Transaction, Inc., from *Successful Schools for Young Adolescents*, by Joan Lipsitz. ©1984 by Transaction, Inc., pp. 168-69.

A positive school culture in the middle grades must include explicit attention to these priorities:

- Commitment to high academic standards which are supported by every member of the school staff and continuously reinforced in daily interactions with students.

- Commitment to high standards of personal and social behavior, jointly defined by administrators, teachers, counselors, parents, and students; these expectations are systematically reinforced in the daily conduct of school activities.

- Strong belief on the part of teachers that they can and do make a difference in the lives of their students. Some researchers call this a "sense of efficacy" and stress that it projects a contagious spirit of optimism which spells the difference between mediocrity and high levels of physical and intellectual energy among both teachers and students.

- Knowledge on the part of all staff members regarding the multiple developmental characteristics of early adolescence; this knowledge is reflected in a pervasive sense of caring which is communicated directly, deliberately, and continuously in all of the teacher-student relationships.

- Acceptance is demonstrated among all staff members regarding the significance of rewards and incentives as responses to student excellence; recognition is provided for all forms of achievement, even though a primary focus on academic accomplishments is maintained.

- Knowledge about the essential qualities of administrative leadership is understood by all members of the faculty. This leadership is characterized by actions which express commitment to common purposes and goals, flexibility, encouragement of autonomy and

Effective Schools

One of the most important achievements of education research in the last 20 years has been indentifying factors that characterize effective schools, in particular the schools that have been especially successful in teaching basic skills to children from low-income families. Analysts first uncovered these characteristics when comparing the achievement levels of students from different urban schools. They labeled the schools with the highest achievement as "effective schools."

Schools with high student achievement and morale show certain characteristics:

- Vigorous instructional leadership,
- A principal who makes clear, consistent, and fair decisions,
- An emphasis on discipline and a safe and orderly environment,
- Instructional practices that focus on basic skills and academic achievement,
- Collegiality among teachers in support of student achievement
- Teachers with high expectations that all their students can and will learn, and
- Frequent review of student progress.

Effective schools are places where principals, teachers, students, and parents agree on the goals, methods, and content of schooling. They are united in recognizing the importance of a coherent curriculum, public recognition for students who succeed, promoting a sense of school pride, and protecting school time for learning.

What Works: Research about Teaching and Learning. Prepared under the direction of William J. Bennett. Washington, D.C.: United States Department of Education, 1986, p. 45.

innovation among teachers, and recognition and respect for their work. It also involves the capacity to delegate and to match individual professional strengths with specific tasks, an intense concern for excellence in teaching and learning, and a strong willingness to engage in collaborative problem solving with faculty members, parents, and students.

There is cause for optimism with respect to the potential of developing high morale in schools which serve the middle grades. The capacity to define the essential characteristics of wholesome school cultures and their demonstrably powerful effects upon students and faculty members represent significant factors in efforts to achieve educational excellence. But there is a chilling effect reflected in events, attitudes, and actions which work against staff morale and, by definition, student morale.

Teachers and principals daily experience the ambiguity and uncertainty of district policies related to middle grade education. They have an increasing sense of the urgency of educational reform in terms of increased expectations for high standards of individual student achievement. They also know that impartial analyses by nationally known experts and professional organizations are singling out the middle grades as the pivot point for millions of the nation's youth – the moment of truth in which intellec-tual values and lifelong academic commitments begin to be shaped.

Yet, these realities are not consistent with the fiscal, political, and administrative status which too many middle grade schools currently experience. There must be new levels of advocacy which will create a fresh image of the middle grade years professionally and politically as a time of intense academic significance for young adolescents.

Administrative, political, and fiscal decisions which reduce uncertainty and ambiguity about the status and priority of middle grade education must be vigorously pursued if the ideal of a positive, student-centered philosophy is to permeate the culture of each school.

TASK FORCE RECOMMENDATIONS

❶ **Superintendents, principals, teachers, and counselors should make use of extensive research findings related to the characteristics of positive school cultures; this use should include systematic analyses of relevant variables and their implications for modifications of policy and practice at district, school, and classroom levels. Research findings focus on the following characteristics:**

a. **Order and purpose represent a clear commitment to the proposition that the professional staff can make a substantive difference in the lives of students; there is a distinct sense of mission which is reflected by this commitment.**

b. **Time is viewed as a finite variable; classrooms are organized and managed to achieve high standards of efficiency.**

c. **Students and teachers are highly interactive; teachers are strongly student-centered in planning and decision making.**

d. **A high level of esprit and enthusiasm exists; teachers, counselors, and principals like young adolescents.**

e. **Organizational health is reflected through principals who "lead" as well as manage.**

f. **Parent and community involvement in the life of the school is welcomed and encouraged.**

❷ **The State Department of Education and local school boards should define administrative and fiscal policies which identify the middle grades as a distinct level of educational experience worthy of separate attention in terms of curriculum, instruction, staffing, financing, and management.**

13 Extracurricular and Intramural Activities

Every middle grade student should have access to extracurricular and intramural programs which develop a sense of personal connectedness to school through activities which promote participation, interaction, competition, and service.

Extracurricular and intramural activities should be open to all middle grade students. Interest clubs, classroom guidance programs, science fairs, pep squads, community projects, in-school scouting programs, intramural sports, academic competitions, and other similar activities have the potential to enable all students to earn and enjoy recognition from both peers and teachers. These satisfactions lead directly to the personal and emotional development of young adolescents – both critical goals of middle grade education.

Participation in extracurricular and intramural activities helps many students, who otherwise experience difficulty in identifying with the academic goals of school, to achieve a sense of "connectedness." For these students a shaky and tenuous relationship can be transformed through the sense of pride which comes from personal accomplishments in school-related programs.

For students who are succeeding academically, involvement in school-sponsored extracurricular and intramural activities is also very important. Their experiences represent a vital counterpoint to their classroom responsibilities and contribute to the goal of full intellectual, social, emotional, and physical development.

For members of the school staff, involvement with students in extracurricular and intramural activities can lead the way to positive encounters with student peer cultures. These experiences build strong bonds between students and staff which spill over into the classroom.

School and bus scheduling must reflect the expectation that all middle grade students will take part in extracurricular and intramural programs. Principals must assume major responsiblity in ensuring that schedules facilitate student participation.

Student Preferences

Middle school students between the ages of 11 and 16 chose athletic games as their favorite social activity in school and selected parties and field days as their second choice, according to a survey by the National Association of Secondary School Principals (NASSP).

The number of students who selected athletic activities declined as students matured. Twelve percent of the 11-year-olds, 10 percent of the 12-year-olds, and 9 percent of the 13-year-olds picked athletic games first, but only 5 percent of the 14-year-olds did so.

The survey of 726 students revealed athletic games to be the most popular with 116 votes. Parties and field day activities, where students participate in races and games, tied for second with 109 votes.

Other choices in the top 10 were: athletic contests, with 80 votes; roller or ice skating, 67; school carnivals, 63; and talent shows, 60.

Respondents were instructed not to select spectator sports, dances, or video games, according to NASSP. The event had to be at school and cost not more than $1 per student.

"Socialization has traditionally been viewed as a primary function of middle level schools—those with sixth through ninth grades," said George Melton, NASSP deputy executive director. "While teachers and administrators handle most of the planning of social activities, we have never seen a large-scale survey of what students desire."

Glenn Maynard, "Middle Level Students Suggest Social Activities," *Schools in the Middle; A Report on Trends and Practices,* (April, 1985), pp. 1-4. This excerpt was adapted for the Middle Grade Task Force Report. Reprinted by permission, National Association of Secondary School Principals.

TASK FORCE RECOMMENDATIONS

① **Local school boards should establish policies related to extracurricular and intramural activities for middle grade students which are consistent with the developmental characteristics of early adolescence.**

② **Principals and other school personnel should ensure that extracurricular and intramural programs are creative, diverse, and open to all students.**

③ **Principals should ensure that school schedules (including bus schedules) are designed to facilitate full student participation in extracurricular and intramural programs.**

④ **Faculties should develop a system of awards for leadership, citizenship, achievement, performance, cooperation, and service which are within the reach of all students.**

⑤ **Teachers should identify students with particular difficulty in establishing a sense of connection with the purpose of schooling; these students should be counseled to take part in extracurricular and intramural activities which provide "alternate connections" to school goals.**

⑥ **Teachers should encourage students who are experiencing academic success to take part in extracurricular and intramural activities as a source of balance which contributes to their full intellectual, social, emotional, and physical development.**

14 Student Accountability

Every middle grade student should be accountable for significant standards of academic excellence and personal behavior.

Middle grade students must experience a schoolwide commitment to high standards of academic excellence and personal behavior. Efforts to legislate these qualities through complicated and often arbitrary rules, regulations, threats, and punishments are in most cases singularly unsuccessful. A far more powerful strategy is found in the use of modeled behavior by teachers and principals who define the tenor and quality of academic expectations and personal behavior through their daily interactions with students and each other.

Students should be involved actively with the professional staff in defining and shaping standards of academic excellence and personal behavior both in and out of the classroom. This means a continuous, positive interaction which gives students a sense of direct participation in creating the qualitative dimensions of their school environment.

There is an inescapable relationship between standards of academic excellence and personal behavior. High levels of achievement are more likely to be sustained in an orderly, secure school in which behavior problems are minimized while the primary energies of students and teachers are devoted to learning tasks.

An orderly and secure learning environment is one of the most important administrative priorities of the principal. Research evidence suggests the significant impact which high standards of student behavior have on academic achievement:

Behavior and academic success go together. In one recent survey, for example, students who got "mostly A's" had one-third as many absences or incidents of tardiness per semester as those who got "mostly D's." The same students were 25 times more likely to have their homework done and 7 times less likely to have been in trouble with the law. Good behavior ... led to better grades and higher achievement. ...[1]

Creating the basis of an orderly and secure learning environment which supports and sustains high standards of academic excellence and personal behavior demands a rational approach to policies, practices, and personal accountability. Several critical factors with a strong empirical basis in school management practices[2] deserve special consideration:

1 *What Works: Research About Teaching and Learning.* Prepared under the direction of William J. Bennett. Washington, D.C.: United States Department of Education, 1986, p. 47.

2 James J. Fenwick, *The Middle School Years.* San Diego, Calif.: Fenwick Associates, ©1986, pp. 46-47.

What Is Real and Possible?

...diverse groups of young adolescents can learn together with one another and with adults in peaceable school communities. ...schooling can be enjoyable and productive for adults and students in the middle grades. ...contrary to prevalent assumptions, young adolescents need not be experienced by adults as an emotionally and physically assaultive age group to be placed on "hold" until they "grow out of it." ...it is possible to gather large numbers of young adolescents together in one building for many hours to satisfy adult expectations about behavioral and intellectual growth. ...it is possible for schools to set norms that young adolescents come to value equally with adults. ...so-called dichotomies like social versus intellectual development and equity versus quality need not be mutually exclusive.

Published by permission of Transaction, Inc., from *Successful Schools for Young Adolescents,* by Joan Lipsitz. ©1984 by Transaction, Inc., p. 202.

- Teacher-student relationships have the essential quality of professional-client interaction as opposed to authoritarian control. School is perceived as a place characterized by cooperation rather than coercion and conflict. Principal-teacher relationships model cooperative behavior and provide the affirmation necessary to allow deeper, more humane interaction between teachers and students.

- Emphasis is on "rules" with a positive cast. These deal with such concepts as excellence, service, creativity, and innovation. Their focus is on building and expanding as opposed to restraining, controlling, limiting, and inhibiting. Students, teachers, counselors, and principals understand that rules are intended to reinforce positive qualities as well as to restrict negative behavior.

- Sanctions are explicit with respect to antisocial behaviors. Enforceable rules are clearly stated and widely communicated; the consequences of infractions are evenly administered.

- Teachers, counselors, and principals stay close to students as people. They strive to understand student values and peer group norms in order to be wise counselors, positive role models, and effective leaders. They avoid behaviors that diminish students. They seek to enhance the self-esteem of all students.

- Academic requirements are balanced against the psychological, social, and physical needs of students. Differences in priorities between students and teachers are recognized, respected, and accommodated. Psychological health, social sensitivity, and physical well-being are accepted as invaluable counterparts of intellectual growth and academic achievement.

- Students are helped to feel secure and to avoid living in fear. They are taught the need for optimism and how to differentiate between real dangers and imagined ones. They are helped to develop positive values and attitudes which ensure physical and emotional well-being. They are enabled to experience the intrinsic rewards that come from

Student Interest and Motivation

I think most parents and other adults would opt for teacher control and dominance in our schools. There has been so much discussion of rebellious youth and of students being "turned off" to school that most people probably support the notion of more authority. However, I suggest that the answer does not lie with more control. The opposite may be true. A large proportion of each data source in our study – parents, teachers, and students – suggested that lack of student interest was a problem at their school. Even though students seemed satisfied with how much decision-making they had and even though they did not see their teachers as authoritarian, I would suggest that a more active role for students in problem solving, decision-making, and in critical thinking activities would cause them to be more motivated and more interested in school.

Kenneth Tye, *The Junior High: A School in Search of a Mission.* Lanham, Md.: University Press of America, Inc., ©1985, p. 343.

expressing care and concern for others.

- Parents support the standards of their schools by reinforcing appropriate student behaviors and academic commitments in the home; they are also prepared to give leadership with respect to educational issues and to provide adequate financial support to their schools.

The relationship between high standards of academic excellence and equally high standards of personal behavior is immediate and direct. When faculties reach out to students with energy, excitement, respect, and creativity, the basis of student accountability for academic excellence and personal behavior becomes visible, symbolic, and powerful in its consequences.

TASK FORCE RECOMMENDATIONS

1 Principals, teachers, counselors, students, and parents should together define the standards of personal behavior which characterize individual and school-level commitments; the following considerations are relevant:

a. Rules are few in number, explicit, comprehensive, and enforceable.

b. Rules are stated positively to the fullest extent possible; emphasis is on desired behavior in contrast to lists of negative behaviors to be avoided.

c. Rules are widely communicated, and the consequences of infractions are quickly and evenly administered among all students.

d. Rules respond to changing circumstances; they are subject continuously to review for their legality, adequacy, relevance, appropriateness, and responsiveness to the best interests of students, faculty, and community.

2 Students and staff should hold each other accountable for high standards of personal conduct and academic excellence; these standards should be reflected by expectations for behavior and achievement which include the following considerations:

Continued on next page

RECOMMENDATIONS *Continued*

a. Students understand the basic relationship between high standards of personal behavior and academic achievement; their daily conduct reflects commitment to this principle.

b. Teachers, counselors, and administrators believe in the capacity of every student to succeed in the core curriculum and share that belief directly with each student in multiple, continuous expressions of affirmation both in words and actions.

c. Teachers believe they can make a difference in what students learn; they experience contagious excitement in helping to develop the emerging intellectual power of young adolescent minds.

d. Academic success is both expected and rewarded. Public recognition is given to students for their accomplishments. Praise-worthy performance is sought in every student, and parents receive frequent communications from teachers and principals regarding the individual successes of students.

e. Incoming students – those transitioning from lower elementary grades and those new to the community – receive special help in identifying with academic standards and individual achievement expectations. Ways are found to assimilate new students into the school's culture and traditions quickly and positively.

f. Teachers, counselors, and principals understand that young adolescents are experiencing rapid developmental changes. Students experience this understanding in multiple ways designed to reduce their anxiety and tension while allowing them to concentrate their intellectual energies on educational goals.

15 Transition

***Every middle grade student should experience a
successful and positive transition among elementary,
middle, and secondary levels of school organization.***

The middle grades are "the in-between years." They serve as a vital link between childhood and older adolescence, which tapers into young adulthood by the time of high school graduation. The philosophy of middle grade education, must, of necessity, deal with the complex interrelationships between intellect and emotions. This agenda represents one of the most persuasive arguments for distinguishing middle grade education as a distinctly unique contribution to the intellectual, emotional, and social development of youth in our society.

It is essential to put the *emotional and social* aspects of transition among different levels of schooling into perspective as a prelude to discussions of *academic* transition. While the academic mission of schools is the predominant concern of educators, young adolescents will respond to that priority in direct proportion to the ability of the school staff to ameliorate their emotional and social anxieties.

Change is threatening at any age. It is especially true for students in transition between the relative security of the early elementary homeroom and the larger, more anonymous setting of the junior high school or middle school. A new school setting, new teachers, new roles, new curricula, and new friends combine to create an environment that at times can become nearly paralyzing in its impact upon students:

Even a successful transition does not necessarily remove continuing elements of personal threat to students throughout their years in the middle grades. The range of issues which students in grades six through eight encounter is astonishing. Many educational sociologists consider the middle grade years to be the most complex social period in the life of an individual. Rapid physical, emotional, and intellectual changes plus an intense preoccupation with questions of personal identity, peer group expectations, and normative values represent compelling challenges.

Recognition of the reality of the threats which students experience is vital. Diminishing these threats is essential. Students should not live in fear—whether of academic failure, low self-esteem, social isolation, or physical harm. This is an absolute in terms of administrative priorities. Ironically, more time may be spent organizationally in ensuring physical safety than in providing emotional security. Both should occupy the same level of concern.[1]

These same concerns exist, even though certain dimensions are different, as students prepare for transition from the middle grades into high school. It is singularly important for teachers and administrators to recognize the perceived threats and pressures which young adolescents anticipate as they prepare to enter high school with large, complex student bodies. The informality of the middle grades will no longer exist. Student hierarchies will be present based on grade-level identification. Exclusive subsets of friends may build impenetrable walls around themselves that

1 James J. Fenwick, *The Middle School Years.* San Diego, Calif.: Fenwick Associates, ©1986, pp. 62-64.

isolate more timid students. Peer group pressures will become even more intense. Those who are adept will find their way. The less secure individuals often falter:

> In most schools for young adolescents, two areas of confusion and ignorance converge: confusion about the purposes of schooling and ignorance about early adolescence as a critical developmental stage in the life span. This unfortunate convergence occurs just at the point in young people's lives when they begin to seek self-definition. It is a dangerous and wasteful situation from which we reap the bitter rewards of apathy, hostility, and rejection.[2]

2 Published by permission of Transaction, Inc., from *Successful Schools for Young Adolescents*, by Joan Lipsitz. ©1984 by Transaction, Inc., p. 171.

Districtwide Transition Panels

The successful transition of students between successive levels of instruction is crucial to their personal, social, and intellectual well-being. The use of "transition panels" is one method for achieving this goal.

Panels are composed of lower elementary, middle, and secondary level teachers, counselors, administrators, and students. Members may represent feeder and receiving schools in a given community or they may be constituted as a district-level panel concerned with communication, articulation, and transition for all students.

Panel agendas should include the continuing review of current transition practices and the degree to which they inhibit or enhance student success. Concerns must include not only transition among student populations which are currently enrolled but must also include the large number of transient students constantly moving among schools and districts.

The primary purpose of transition panels should be to make specific policy recommendations to district superintendents and local boards which are designed to facilitate the easy movement of students among levels of instruction and among schools. Conventional types of recommendations should be accentuated by innovative concepts which selected schools might pilot. Research into successful practices of other districts should be a function of the transition panel, as well. The role of the transition panel is ongoing. Change and movement are constants in the lives of students, their families, and communities. The creative work of those who serve on transition panels can mean the difference between success or failure for many students.

The middle grades must be transitional and organized to allow a gradual and successful movement from early elementary education to high school. Extended blocks of instructional time in selected core curriculums taught by individual teachers or teams of teachers should be a common practice. Specialist teachers should instruct the remaining core curriculum subjects as well as elective and exploratory curricula.

The philosophical and practical intent of this strategy is to allow middle grade students to continue to experience the emotional security of a quasi-homeroom environment for a portion of the day while learning how to interact with gradually larger numbers of teachers, each with unique sets of professional expectations. The concept of "teacher specialist" as opposed to "teacher generalist" is also introduced at this time. These provisions address both the intellectual and emotional needs of students without compromising either.

The fact that middle grade instruction should prepare students for transition to a successful high school experience does not lead to the conclusion that schools which serve the middle grades should be organized as miniature high schools. Such organization may more effectively serve the ego needs of professionals than the emotional and intellectual needs of young adolescents.

It is paradoxical that secondary patterns of school organization tend to dominate education in the upper elementary grades. The same logic would suggest that juniors and seniors in high school should experience the relative freedom and flexibility of the comparatively looser structure of college and university schedules as a necessary preparation for transition to higher education. Multiple national studies of high school education show that just the opposite is true.

High schools have their unique educational mission. High school administrators resent and resist suggestions that high schools should be cast in the mold of higher education – and correctly so.

The same logic allows us to argue for the unique mission of middle grade education. While the academic agendas of the two institutions intersect in terms of an articulated core curriculum continuum, schools which serve the middle grades provide for a critical period of educational transition for young adolescents and should cast their own organizational shadow over the lives of students.

Lipsitz comments:

We are witnessing a policy shift in schooling for young adolescents that is generally unacknowledged. Part of the public's confusion about the trend toward middle schools is the absence of public discourse about whether middle schools are meant to extend the elementary years upward, thereby prolonging childhood, or are meant to extend the secondary years downward, thereby acknowledging and perhaps encouraging the earlier emergence of adolescent capabilities and behavior ... staff members ... say they are doing both, and that this is exactly what it means to be a middle school.[3]

Instructional organization for grades 6, 7, and 8 should provide for an orderly educational transition based on the developmental characteristics of young adolescents. This includes extended blocks of instructional time which approximate in part the home-room environment of the primary grades while gradually moving students into more specialized classes that increasingly resemble the departmentalized structure of the high school.

For example:

- The sixth grade should ideally provide for as many as four core curriculum subjects taught in an extended instructional time block by an individual teacher or a teaching team; the balance of the curriculum should be taught by a combination of either generalists or specialists. Extended instructional time blocks can include reading/literature/language arts/history/geography; mathematics and science; or other logical course combinations based on the skills of teachers and/or teaching teams.

- The seventh grade should allow for a humanities emphasis involving up to three core curriculum subjects taught in an extended instructional time block by an individual teacher or teaching team; the balance of the curriculum should be taught by teacher specialists in separate courses. The extended instructional time block can include reading/literature/

3 Published by permission of Transaction, Inc., from *Successful Schools for Young Adolescents*, by Joan Lipsitz, ©1984 by Transaction, Inc., p.173.

language arts/history/geography; mathematics/science; or other logical course combinations based on the skills of teachers and/or teaching teams.

- The eighth grade should allow for a humanities emphasis involving two or more core curriculum areas taught in an extended instructional time block by an individual teacher or teaching team with the balance of the curriculum taught by teacher specialists in separate courses. The extended instructional time block might include reading/literature/language arts/history/geography; mathematics/science; or other logical combinations of courses based on the skills of teachers and/or teaching teams.

- A vital transitional thread should run through each of the middle grade years in the form of an adviser-advisee program. In its ideal design this program allows a teacher adviser to follow the same students for all three of their middle grade years.

- The concept of extended instructional time blocks for core curriculum subjects provides the opportunity for integrating skills and knowledge across subject-matter lines. Students also have sufficient time to know one another well, to establish close bonds with one or more teachers, and to engage in "active learning" experiences as they pursue curriculum goals and objectives.

- The use of teaching teams in a core curriculum instructional block represents a significant staffing option. Strategically, it provides maximum flexibility for intraclass grouping and regrouping according to individual student learning requirements. The team concept also allows students to experience the combined skills and knowledge of two or more teachers, including the potential for a dynamic, synergistic instructional effect.

- The option of collaborative teaching can be provided as an alternative to team teaching. The same group of stu-

A Model of K-12 Instructional Organization

K-3	4-5	6-8	9-12
Self-contained classrooms taught by a single teacher	Self-contained classrooms taught by a single teacher which include the majority of core curriculum subjects plus teacher specialists for courses in selected subjects within/without the core curriculum	Transition to extended blocks of instructional time involving selected core-curriculum subjects taught by single teachers or teams of teachers using interdisciplinary content designs, when appropriate; specialists teach other core curriculum subjects and elective/exploratory courses	departmentalized organization

core-curriculum continuum

dents is taught by two or more teachers who do not plan their instruction as a team. The major benefit is the cohesiveness of the student group. The major disadvantage is the absence of integrated and/or interdisciplinary instruction, which is one of the hallmarks of team instruction.

- Group guidance programs should be viewed as an invaluable part of the curriculum during each of the middle grade years. These programs can assume various configurations. One of the most popular is the cross-age "advisory" concept which brings small groups of students and teachers together across age-grade boundaries. Students focus on school-related issues and, in the process, build strong bonds of friendship, including the corollaries of trust, group cohesiveness, school spirit, and shared academic goals.

The actual physical act of transition among grade levels is very important. The better the transition is planned and carried out between the lower elementary grades and the middle grades, and between the middle grades and high school, the more academically, emotionally, and socially competent students are likely to become at each level.

The dependent learner of the early elementary grades becomes the independent learner who moves

Representative Features of a Middle Grade "Advisory" or Extended Guidance Program

Sixth Grade
I. Orientation to Middle School
  A. Building
  B. Staff
  C. School rules and student handbook
  D. Student schedule
  E. Individual concerns – sharing
II. Study and Listening Skills
  A. Note taking
  B. Outlining
  C. Library
  D. Homework
  E. Test taking
III. Looking at Ourselves
  A. Acceptance of self
    1. Knowledge of physical changes
    2. Knowledge of emotional changes
    3. Knowledge of social changes
    4. Knowledge of intellectual changes
  B. Personal strengths and weaknesses

Seventh Grade
I. Understanding Myself
  A. Awareness
    1. Words to describe our feelings
    2. Expression of feelings
    3. Self-disclosure
  B. Development of desirable personality traits
    1. Self-confidence
    2. Self-control
    3. Independence
    4. Trust
    5. Respect for others
    6. Appreciation of others
    7. Affection
II. Understanding Others
  A. Awareness of other people's feelings

  B. How behavior affects relationships with others
    1. Family
    2. Friends
    3. Teachers
    4. Classmates
III. Awareness of Values
  A. Understanding values
  B. Exploring personal values
  C. Exploring social values
    1. Honesty
    2. Prejudice
    3. Loyalty
    4. Personal standards
    5. Responsibility
IV. Decision Making
  A. Steps in decision making
  B. Personal decision making
  C. Group decision making

Eighth Grade
I. Decision Making Related to Careers
  A. Review of steps in decision making
II. Goal Setting
  A. Steps in goal setting
  B. Examining types of goals
    1. Long-term
    2. Short-term
  C. The relationship between goals
III. Interests Related to Careers
  A. Interest survey
  B. Utilization of ideas
  C. Characteristics of careers
IV. Abilities Related to Careers
  A. Review of test data
  B. Relationship between abilities and career choices
V. Aptitudes Related to Careers
  A. An overview of aptitudes
  B. Relationship between aptitudes and worker traits
VI. Relating School Subjects to Careers
VII. Individual Projects

Robert Schockley, Richard Schumacher, and Denis Smith, "Teacher Advisory Programs – Strategies for Successful Implementation," *NASSP Bulletin*, Vol. 68 (September, 1984), p. 71, ©1984.

more surely and confidently into high school. The middle grades broker this transition through their special provision for the intellectual, emotional, social, and physical needs of preadolescent and early adolescent students.

TASK FORCE RECOMMENDATIONS

1 Local school boards should establish district policies which formally recognize the unique and substantive mission of middle grade education; care should be taken to define middle grade education on its own terms as opposed to the use of comparisons, metaphors, and organizational patterns appropriate to other levels of education.

2 Superintendents should ensure that an orderly transition occurs between the lower elementary grades, the middle grades, and high school. Variables which should be addressed at the middle grade level are:

a. Gradual movement from primary self-contained classrooms to secondary departmentalized instruction should be emphasized through provision of extended blocks of instructional time devoted to selected core curriculum subjects.

b. Adviser-advisee programs should be provided which build strong student-teacher relationships; the teacher adviser should follow the same students throughout their middle grade years.

c. Group guidance programs should be designed to build strong, positive peer group relationships; special consideration should be given to developing shared values and goals, including personal

Continued on next page

RECOMMENDATIONS *Continued*

commitments to academic achievement prior to entry into high school.

③ Principals, counselors, and teachers from sending and receiving schools should plan and implement strategies which facilitate an orderly, enjoyable, and successful transition for students between schools. Strategies include:

a. On-site visitations for students to their new school prior to their actual transfer.

b. Faculty collaboration between sending and receiving schools regarding logistical details; each student's needs should be anticipated, including those which relate to transportation, payment of fees, course scheduling, and other similar matters.

c. Provision of older student mentors who help new students to adapt quickly to new rules and routines and to meet new friends.

d. Student-parent orientations, newsletters, and other types of school-home communications.

e. Assurances that every incoming student is known by name by one or more teachers and counselors on the first day of the new school assignment.

16 Structure

Middle grade education should be identified with grades 6, 7, and 8; disparities in state funding formulas among elementary, high school, and unified school districts should be eliminated for these grades.

The identification and organization of the middle grades in terms of schools enrolling students in grades 6, 7, and 8 is recommended for the following essential reasons:

- Developmentally, students in grades 6, 7, and 8 have more in common in terms of physical, psychological, social, and intellectual variables than do those in other age-grade combinations.

- Fifth grade students typically have not yet crossed the threshold of early adolescence. Their developmental readiness is more closely linked with students in grade 4.

- Ninth grade students tend to identify emotionally and intellectually with students in grades 10 through 12.

- The organization of secondary curriculum sequences logically follows a four-year pattern and corresponds to the needs of students to satisfy college entrance requirements.

- A three-year middle grade time frame allows the opportunity for strong, positive relationships to be built among students, teachers, counselors, and administrators; this bonding is critical to healthy intellectual and emotional development and sets the stage for future academic success and personal/social development for young adolescents.

Those who argue that the nature and quality of middle grade education are more critical than a given configuration of grades are correct. There may be powerful local constraints which preclude a 6–8 grade organization in some districts. The result will be an alternative configuration more in keeping with the unique needs of individual communities.

However, school districts which must operate schools within other grade level configurations do not need to sacrifice or compromise the goals of middle grade educational

Personalized Environment in Exemplary Schools

...Young adolescents are not ready for the atomistic independence foisted on them in secondary schools, which is one of the causes of the behavior problems endemic to many junior high schools. Behavior problems lead to omnipresent control mechanisms, resulting in the dissonant combination of an overdose of both unearned independence and overbearing regulations. Young adolescents are told, incorrectly, that they are adults, and then infantilized when they do not measure up. [Middle] schools grant more independence than elementary schools do, while establishing strong support groups (houses, teams, wings, advisory groups). Gradually, students gain increasing amounts of independence. They remain, however, in a highly personalized environment. The nature of the schools' organizational structure establishes continuity in adult-child relationships and opportunities for the lives of students and adults to cross in mutually meaningful ways. In each school, students express their appreciation for being cared about and known. They are actively aware of being liked, which is notable only because, in most schools, young adolescents are generally disliked.

Published by permission of Transaction, Inc., from *Successful Schools for Young Adolescents,* by Joan Lipsitz, ©1984 by Transaction, Inc., p. 181.

reform defined in this report. Creative scheduling designs and related school management practices have the capacity to allow each substantive recommendation to be fully implemented within any type of school organization which includes grades 6, 7, and 8.

Many aspects of structural change in the middle grades can be accomplished through the modification of changes in policies and practices and the reallocation of existing resources. Such efforts require creative efforts on the part of board members, superintendents, principals, and teachers. Other reform goals can be achieved only through the provision of major new fiscal resources.

The state Legislature should elevate middle grade education to a much higher level of priority. Of particular urgency are the present disparities in state funding formulas for the middle grades among elementary, high school, and unified school districts. These disparities must be addressed and resolved.

The characteristics of middle grade organization have been extensively researched. Data strongly suggest that changing to a middle school philosophy and organizational pattern positively affects such variables as student achievement, personal development, learning climate, faculty morale, staff development, and parental and community involvement.

Research, reported by the Association for Supervision and Curriculum Development (ASCD), has identified the degree to which

Beyond Team Teaching: The Urgency of Team Organization in the Middle Grades

One of the most important developments in the capacity of the middle school to organize in a way that meets, simultaneously, the needs for learning and socialization was the painful but profitable realization that team teaching and interdisciplinary team organization are not synonymous. For decades, stretching back to the beginning of the junior high school at the turn of the century, middle level educators had admirably attempted to institute a variety of team teaching programs. These attempts were made in the belief (probably correct) that the students could learn in far more meaningful ways when the subjects in the curriculum were presented to them in thematically interwoven units. Teachers were trained and encouraged to plan collaboratively, time and money were devoted to the creation of units, parents were advised of the new learning experiences their children would be enjoying, and the students eagerly anticipated an excitingly different educational program....

Educators have learned that the interdisciplinary team organization is far more than a way to encourage team teaching. It is a method of bringing teachers and students together to establish authentic learning communities, not just an administrative technique to get something else accomplished. When teachers and students are grouped together into interdisciplinary teams it creates an educational glue that holds together almost every other aspect of the school program.

The interdisciplinary team organization is based on sharing (Alexander and George, 1981). Teachers and students share, first of all, each other. The teachers on the team all teach the same students, and the students on the team have the same teachers in the basic academic program. Teachers and students also share, to the degree possible, the same basic physical area of the school and the same schedule. Without this organized sharing, there is no team, and without the team, the opportunity for a sense of community is lost.

An interdisciplinary team is, then, a group of teachers, usually from two to five persons representing the basic academic subjects, who share the same students, the same space, and the same schedule. On some teams teachers may share the responsibility for teaching the basic subjects to the students, in some form of team teaching, but frequently this is not the case. More often, teachers on teams share an interest in the total academic program in which their common students are involved.

The most absolutely essential thing is that teachers share the same students and have the opportunity to work together with the needs of those common students in mind. Being right next door, across the hall, or in the same pod is almost as essential. Teachers who do not share the same students have little reason to work

Continued on next page

2 Paul S. George and Lynn L. Oldaker, "A National Survey of Middle School Effectiveness," *Educational Leadership*, Vol. 42. (December, 1985/January, 1986), p. 79. Reprinted with permission of the Association for Supervision and Curriculum Development. ©1986 by the Association for Supervision and Curriculum Development. All rights reserved.

programs of exemplary schools could be deemed to be effective for the education of early adolescents. The most striking findings to emerge include:

- *Ninety percent [of the schools] organized teachers and students into interdisciplinary teams, rather than self-contained and departmentalized instruction.*

- *Ninety-four percent used flexible scheduling during the school day, often with some kind of block schedule.*

- *Ninety-three percent [of the schools] included a home base period and teacher-adviser for each student.*

- *All of the respondents said their programs were designed with the nature of middle school students in mind.*

- *Ninety-nine percent focused curriculum on students' personal development and skills for continued learning and a wide range of exploratory activities.*

- *All reported that administrators and faculty members collaborated on decisions that shaped school policy.[2]*

In separate research findings, Lipsitz's analysis of successful schools led her to the conclusion that *"The individual decisions made by each school reflect ... thoughtful response to the developmental needs of the age group and the particular needs of the school's clientele."*

She continues:

Underlying their varied responses is a commitment to the intellectual, social, and personal growth of each child. While such a statement is identical to the standard rhetoric of schools, it is as close to fact in these schools as is possible in a less than perfect social institution. Important factors contributing to the schools' climate appear to be the physical setting, the means by which order is achieved, teachers' working conditions, their beliefs and expectations, and the acknowledgment of reciprocity in human relations. Crucially important are the quality of leadership and the clarity of purpose already discussed.[3]

There are multiple issues which should be addressed in structuring effective middle grade education:

- Large schools need to be divided into smaller, more easily managed units. Whether called "houses," "school-within-a-school," or by some other term, the primary purpose is to allow a sense of closeness to develop between students and staff which enhances the development of intellectual growth, academic achievement, and emotional and social maturity.

- Smaller administrative units within a school can be organized by grade level or cross-graded. Whatever combination is used, care must be taken to ensure a balance among the variables that characterize the diversity of given student body populations; ethnic, linguistic, and socioeconomic diversity as well as other individual qualities which lend vitality and interest to human relationships must be protected in the process of creating smaller administrative units.

- Instruction can be organized in terms of time blocks that facilitate multiple goals, including extended units of time for teaching selected core curriculum subjects through interdisciplinary approaches by individual teachers or teams.

- Classroom-based guidance activities should be an integral part of the middle grade program. Every teacher should be guidance oriented and sensitive to adolescent developmental characteristics; this professional frame of reference can markedly diminish individual and group stress levels and maximize the use of student energies for learning purposes.

- Curriculum organization and course scheduling should facilitate schoolwide planning among teachers, irrespective of subject-area assignments.

- Schoolwide reading and writing programs should be planned and implemented which cut through all core and exploratory curriculums. Every teacher and student should become involved. The more able student readers and writers should be pushed toward advanced levels of literacy while those in need of basic skills help should receive specialized assistance.

- Teachers should be provided with common planning time when their instructional responsibilities require coordination.

- "Advisory" programs should be included in the organization of the middle grades. This concept is well documented as a cost-efficient means of developing bridges between students and staff. Small groups of students in cross-age groupings engage in shared experiences that build morale, enhance school spirit, develop

3 Published by permission of Transaction, Inc., from *Successful Schools for Young Adolescents*, by Joan Lipsitz, ©1984 by Transaction, Inc., pp. 178-79.

positive educational values, and improve achievement levels.

• District offices should be organized to provide direct support services related to middle grade curriculum, instruction, staffing, and other administrative requirements. In larger districts, middle grade administrative units should be established for this purpose.

• Adequate physical plant facilities must be provided for middle grade schools. An "active learning" instructional philosophy for the core and exploratory curricula can be achieved only when space allocations allow for a wide variety of specialized instructional experiences. The same argument is advanced with respect to the need for adequate equipment and instructional materials, including cutting edge educational technology.

Provision must be made within the State Department of Education for middle grade support services. An administrative unit specifically assigned to this mission must be created.

TASK FORCE RECOMMENDATIONS

❶ Superintendents and principals should ensure that the concept of _team organization_ characterizes and permeates the structure of middle grade schools. Specifically, teachers should:

a. Share the same students as extensively as possible.

b. Work together with the needs of those common students in mind.

❷ The state Legislature, with the support of the Governor and the Superintendent of Public Instruction, should resolve state-level funding disparities among elementary, high school, and unified school districts which negatively impact fiscal resources available for grades 6, 7, and 8.

❸ The state Legislature, with the support of the Governor and the Superintendent of Public Instruction, should amend recently adopted school facilities' legislation:

Continued on next page

RECOMMENDATIONS *Continued*

a. **To eliminate fiscal incentives for building 7–9 schools.**

b. **To eliminate disincentives for building 6–8 schools.**

c. **To alter the square foot allocation formula so that the square footage for grade 6 is the same as that for grades 7 and 8 in schools which contain grades 6, 7, and 8.**

❹ **The Legislature, with the support of the Governor, and the Superintendent of Public Instruction, should adopt legislation designed to encourage improvements in middle grade education. The School Improvement Program Law should be amended to:**

a. **Require participating schools which enroll students in grades 6, 7, and/or 8 to consider the recommendations of this report in their respective school planning processes.**

b. **Encourage a planning focus for grades 6, 7, and 8, regardless of the grade-level configuration of individual schools, in addition to schoolwide planning which may involve other grade levels.**

c. **Require unification of school planning processes for all federal, state, and local programs in each curriculum area in order to ensure that all resources are directed to helping students succeed in the core curriculum, to the extent allowable under applicable statutes.**

d. **Encourage allocation of state and local Economic Impact Aid funds to services designed to increase the number of under-represented minorities preparing for high**

Continued on next page

RECOMMENDATIONS *Continued*

school courses required for admission to four-year institutions of higher education.

e. Encourage budgeting of School Improvement Program, categorical, and local district funds in support of the implementation of individual school plans in response to this report.

f. Appropriate funds and revise existing formulas to allow expansion of the School Improvement Program to all schools which enroll students in grades 6, 7, and 8 over the next three years.

⑤ Local school boards should adopt policies that identify middle grade education with grades 6, 7, and 8; local boards should ensure that middle grade schools are provided with appropriate space and specialized facilities essential for achieving stated educational and organizational objectives, including:

a. Interdisciplinary team teaching in core curriculum instructional time blocks

b. Flexible scheduling of class time according to particularized requirements of different curriculums

c. Active learning environments which require access to multiple types of facilities, including laboratories, studios, performing arts facilities, media centers, large- and small-group classrooms, convertible rooms, gyms, and other comparable facilities

⑥ The State Department of Education should establish a special instructional support unit for middle grade education.

⑦ Local school boards should authorize separate, specialized central office support services for

Continued on next page

RECOMMENDATIONS *Continued*

schools which enroll students in the middle grades.

⑧ Superintendents and building administrators should provide leadership in developing organizational principles for the middle grades which incorporate the following:

a. Large schools should be divided into smaller, more easily managed administrative units.

b. These smaller administrative units should reflect the full range of student diversity found within the total school population.

c. Instructional time should be allocated on the basis of relative priorities among subject areas; given classes may meet daily, alternatively by day or week, and for varied lengths of time.

d. All students should have one-to-one access to a significant adult through adviser-advisee programs, conventional counseling, and/or other comparable programs.

e. Multiple types of teaching arrangements should be made possible in response to individual student needs, teacher preferences, and the requirements of specific courses, including, but not limited to, core curriculum teaching teams, collaborative teaching, teacher-counselor teams, specialist teacher assignments in selected subjects, remedial instruction in basic skills, accelerated instruction for gifted classes, self-contained classes, and independent study programs.

f. Schoolwide reading and writing programs should be incorporated within the core curriculum for all students.

g. "Advisory" programs should become a standard feature of middle grade education.

17 Scheduling: An Expression of Middle Grade Philosophy

The school schedule for the middle grades should be a direct reflection of a sound educational philosophy and should facilitate equal access by all students to the full range of instructional programs and student support services.

The most basic expression of a school's philosophy is found in its master schedule. Profound and noble expressions of educational goals and commitments can be compromised — even abandoned — when the master schedule fails to respond creatively to them.

The master schedule must facilitate every student's ability to realize the full benefits of a school's program. It should enable coherent, rational planning. The loss of ability to exercise a given course option by a student should never be directly attributable to ill-conceived scheduling.

The subject of master scheduling has received far too little attention. Time is finite. The length of the school day and school year have changed little in the past one hundred years. Yet, in that same period, the knowledge base has grown exponentially. In addition, the magnitude of expectations which society holds for the public schools relative to other than academic responsibilities has grown phenomenally.

Added to these variables are those which relate to curricular and instructional innovations which hold out new hope to countless students. At the middle grade level these

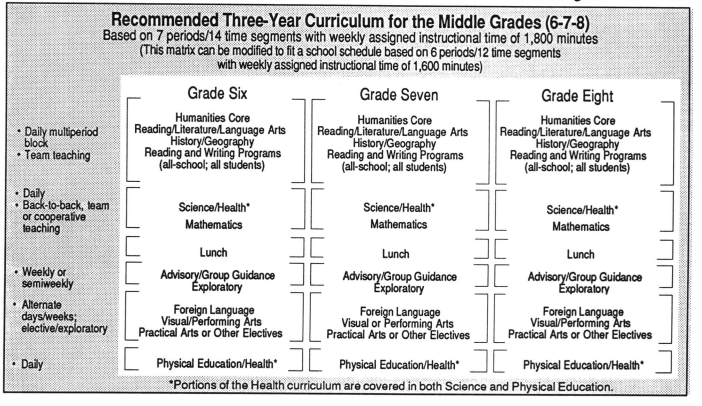

Recommended Three-Year Curriculum for the Middle Grades (6-7-8)
Based on 7 periods/14 time segments with weekly assigned instructional time of 1,800 minutes
(This matrix can be modified to fit a school schedule based on 6 periods/12 time segments
with weekly assigned instructional time of 1,600 minutes)

	Grade Six	Grade Seven	Grade Eight
• Daily multiperiod block • Team teaching	Humanities Core Reading/Literature/Language Arts History/Geography Reading and Writing Programs (all-school; all students)	Humanities Core Reading/Literature/Language Arts History/Geography Reading and Writing Programs (all-school; all students)	Humanities Core Reading/Literature/Language Arts History/Geography Reading and Writing Programs (all-school; all students)
• Daily • Back-to-back, team or cooperative teaching	Science/Health* Mathematics	Science/Health* Mathematics	Science/Health* Mathematics
	Lunch	Lunch	Lunch
• Weekly or semiweekly	Advisory/Group Guidance Exploratory	Advisory/Group Guidance Exploratory	Advisory/Group Guidance Exploratory
• Alternate days/weeks; elective/exploratory	Foreign Language Visual/Performing Arts Practical Arts or Other Electives	Foreign Language Visual or Performing Arts Practical Arts or Other Electives	Foreign Language Visual/Performing Arts Practical Arts or Other Electives
• Daily	Physical Education/Health*	Physical Education/Health*	Physical Education/Health*

*Portions of the Health curriculum are covered in both Science and Physical Education.

include such considerations as interdisciplinary teaching, cooperative teaching, peer tutoring, team planning, independent study, "advisory" classes, individualized counseling, active learning, mentoring – the list seems endless.

Can the multiplicity of goals expected in effective middle grade schooling be achieved? The answer must be "yes"! Whatever is educationally correct must become administratively possible. But constraints do exist. The dependent and independent variables must be realistically accounted for in the design of scheduling algorithms. A school staff must know what its most basic commitments are. These represent the heart of a philosophical statement which the master schedule must articulate.

Lipsitz has valuable insight to offer at this point:

The lesson about structure is seen in words like organic and evolving... Organizational decisions resulted from school philosophy. School philosophy is deeply influenced by sensitivity to the age group. It is also influenced by the personalities of talented leaders and a core group of highly dedicated teachers responding to the clamorous demands of a group of students whose energies they enjoy and wish to promote.[1]

The following principles are essential in guiding scheduling decisions in the middle grades:

- The school schedule must reflect the school philosophy and must be considered as the most basic administrative instrument for translating philosophy into action.

- The school schedule must be the product of professional collaboration and reflect an expression of consensus among staff, students, and parents regarding relative program priorities.

- The school schedule must be thought of as dynamic, alterable, and always subordinate to changing requirements of students and faculty.

Related to these principles are multiple logistical considerations. Schedules for the middle grades must make provision for:

- Extended blocks of uninterrupted instructional time for selected core curriculum courses with the option for interdisciplinary content design.

- Exploratory courses which allow students to experience new categories of skills and knowledge and to pursue special interests.

- Options for team, collaborative, and independent self-contained teaching modes.

- Teacher planning time, including common periods for members of teaching teams.

- Equal access to all instructional programs by all students at any time dependent on individual readiness levels.

- Determination of course offerings and their allocated times during the school day on the basis of a systematic analysis of student program forecasts

1 Published by permission of Transaction, Inc., from *Successful Schools for Young Adolescents*, by Joan Lipsitz, ©1984 by Transaction, Inc., p. 193.

in contrast to random determinations based solely on assumptions related to prior administrative experience and practice.

- Integration of course schedules when schools are divided into "units" or similar administrative arrangements in order to facilitate maximum access by students to exploratory subjects which may be taught only once or twice daily.

- Student advisory programs, including allowance for optimum grouping of both students and staff members.

- Group guidance, student government, mentoring, peer and cross-age tutoring, and other specialized programs which are minimally disruptive of assigned instructional time.

- Accomplishment of necessary logistical tasks (attendance, lunch counts, school announcements, etc.) in "home rooms" or "reg rooms" prior to the beginning of the regular instructional day.

- Implementation of an "active learning" philosophy, including easy access by students and teachers to school-based learning resources which include a library, media center, labs, studios, small-group work areas, independent

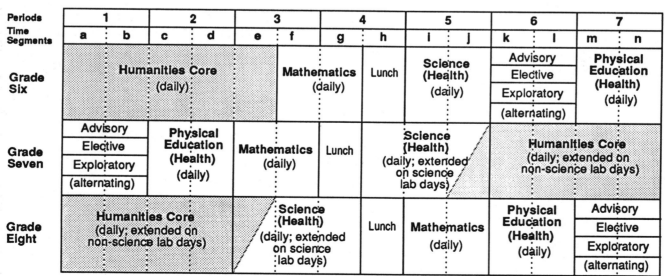

A Proposed Schedule Matrix for the Middle Grades (6-7-8)

Based on 7 periods/14 time segments with weekly assigned instructional time of 1,800 minutes
(This matrix can be modified to fit a school schedule based on 6 periods/12 time segments with weekly assigned instructional time of 1,600 minutes)

Periods	1		2		3		4		5		6		7	
Time Segments	a	b	c	d	e	f	g	h	i	j	k	l	m	n
Grade Six	Humanities Core (daily)				Mathematics (daily)		Lunch		Science (Health) (daily)		Advisory / Elective / Exploratory (alternating)		Physical Education (Health) (daily)	
Grade Seven	Advisory / Elective / Exploratory (alternating)		Physical Education (Health) (daily)		Mathematics (daily)		Lunch		Science (Health) (daily; extended on science lab days)		Humanities Core (daily; extended on non-science lab days)			
Grade Eight	Humanities Core (daily; extended on non-science lab days)				Science (Health) (daily; extended on science lab days)		Lunch		Mathematics (daily)		Physical Education (Health) (daily)		Advisory / Elective / Exploratory (alternating)	

The use of multiple time segments dramatically increases scheduling flexibility. It allows for a broader range of instructional strategies to be employed. It allows differentiation to occur in terms of instructional time allocated to specific subjects. It enables provision of a broader, richer array of exploratory subjects without compromising the priority of the core curriculum. It facilitates group guidance activities plus offering multiple other benefits.

Fenwick Associates (1986)

study facilities, and other comparable resources.

- Varied lengths of instructional time assigned to different courses on the basis of predefined learning goals; the requirements of laboratory courses vary significantly from those where no set-up or put-away time is involved; the goal should be that of addressing the amount of time-on-task as opposed to assigned class time.

- Periodic review of all courses to evaluate the adequacy of both assigned instructional time and physical facilities in relation to stated curriculum goals; disparities should be addressed and resolved.

- Innovation and experimentation with varied time configurations; the school day must be thought of as a finite number of hours and minutes divisible by any number capable of creating viable blocks of time of varied lengths and allocated on the basis of course priorities and instructional requirements.

- Innovation and experimentation with varied configurations of weekly, monthly, or semester-length blocks of time. Courses must be evaluated in terms of whether or not daily instruction is required or whether course lengths can be altered without compromising the curricular goals.

- Use of commercially available software to schedule complex program requirements.

The dominant theme is flexibility. The school schedule should be dynamic, alterable, and always subordinate to the changing requirements of students and faculty. Lipsitz captures the essence of flexibility which the middle grade schedule should allow:

Finally, the schools are willing, indeed eager, to modify or overthrow the schedule for part of a day, a full day, a week, a session of the year, or for an ad hoc special event, to discourage the monotony of routine endemic to all schools.[2]

The range of program expectations in the middle grades is

[2] Published by permission of Transaction, Inc., from *Successful Schools for Young Adolescents,* by Joan Lipsitz, ©1984 by Transaction, Inc., p. 194.

Innovative Scheduling

Willard Junior High School in Berkeley, California, has developed a unique and effective procedure for providing extra instructional support for compensatory education students. A special period has been inserted in the daily schedule between 10:25 and 11:00 a.m. during which students get advanced instructional help on assignments they will receive the following week in their regular, heterogeneously grouped English classes.

For example, if the assigned reading in the regular class is *To Kill a Mockingbird,* compensatory education students might receive prior help in defining the plot, identifying the major characters, and developing new vocabulary related to the assignment.

The Willard project demonstrates the way in which substantive compensatory education can be creatively provided without pulling students out of their core curriculum classes. Even more significantly, this type of specialized assistance has enabled compensatory education students to keep up with their peers in heterogeneously grouped English classes. Three years of experience document the success of the program.

During the same daily timeframe, the Underrepresented College Opportunity (UCO) and Gifted and Talented Education (GATE) programs provide specialized instructional support for eligible students – again without drawing them away from full participation in their regular core curriculum classes.

extensive. In some instances, in spite of the best efforts, serious logistical problems will remain to be solved. Schools which are willing to explore innovative scheduling options should be encouraged to do so. The extension of the length of the instructional day for middle grade students is specifically recommended. State and local district fiscal incentives should be provided in instances where added resources have the potential to impact significantly the successful implementation of core curriculum offerings and creative instructional practices.

TASK FORCE RECOMMENDATIONS

❶ Principals, teachers, and counselors should draw on a carefully defined school philosophy in determining school scheduling priorities; program requirements should drive all scheduling decisions. Examples include:

a. Extended time blocks for selected core curriculum classes

b. Differentiated assignments of instructional time based on the nature of the subject (e.g., laboratory versus expository instruction)

c. Alternated time to allow a broader range of learning experiences within fixed time constraints (e.g., classes which meet every day, alternate days, alternate weeks, alternate semesters, or other variations, as appropriate)

d. Elective/exploratory course options

e. Shared planning time for teachers who team or collaborate

f. Schedule planning for all teachers

g. Allocated time for counseling and guidance programs; options to be accommodated within a common alternating time block include possibilities such as:

- **Adviser-advisee programs**
- **Group guidance activities**
- **Tutorials and mentoring sessions for**

Continued on next page

RECOMMENDATIONS *Continued*

special groups of students (e.g., underrepresented minorities, gifted; basic skills deficient; limited-English proficient, and others).

h. Shortened or otherwise modified activity schedules to enable assemblies or other special events to occur without canceling regularly scheduled classes.

❷ Principals, teachers, and counselors should view the school schedule as dynamic, alterable, and always subordinate to changing program requirements.

❸ The State Department of Education, the California League of Middle Schools (CLMS), the Association of California School Administrators (ACSA), and the California Association for Counseling and Development (CACD) should provide assistance to principals, teachers, and counselors on the theory and design of middle grade schedules through provision of models, simulations, software applications, planning seminars, and related types of resources.

❹ The State Department of Education and local school boards should encourage major innovations in middle grade scheduling practices; policies and administrative guidelines should be provided which allow maximum flexibility in designing schedules in order to accommodate successfully multiple program demands.

❺ The state Legislature, with the support of the Governor, should expand financial incentives for schools (districts) which extend the length of the middle grade instructional day or which engage in special innovative scheduling practices which require significant additional expenditures.

18 Assessment

Assessment programs for the middle grades should be comprehensive; they should include measurement of a broad range of educational goals related to student achievement and program effectiveness; the primary purposes of middle grade assessment should be to compile data which lead to improved curriculum and instructional programs and more effective student support services.

The primary goal of strong middle grade assessment practices is to provide data which will lead to improved curriculum and instructional programs and more effective student support services. There are multiple principles of middle grade education presented in this report. These principles are, in fact, goal statements which can be reduced to measurable objectives. These objectives have the capacity to become the basis for designing an assessment program with direct meaning for those involved at every level of middle grade educational reform.

Valid assessment practices should enable those responsible for middle grade educational policies at state, county, and local district levels to examine their philosophical commitments and administrative actions. Measurement feedback should be provided which allows for a logical, systematic evaluation of these critical variables.

This type of analysis has the capacity to enable policymakers, administrators, and teachers to resolve differences, achieve new levels of unanimity of purpose, and to commit together to new levels of involvement in middle grade reform efforts.

Some of the objectives implicit in the principles contained in this report will be more difficult to measure than others. These include those which relate directly to more complex student learning outcomes. For the most part, standardized testing programs focus on a more narrow, tightly defined range of knowledge and skills than those emphasized in our recommendations. The Carnegie Report captures the essence of the issues involved in shifting from old priorities to new types of learning outcomes which will require significant changes in evaluation practices:

... Over the last few years, many schools have demonstrated significant gains in student performance on standardized test scores and other measures of basic competence. But, at the same time, too many students lack the ability to reason and perform complex, nonroutine intellectual tasks. We are doing better on the old goals, often at the expense of making progress on the goals that count the most. Because we have defined the problem of the schools in terms of decline from earlier standards, we have unwittingly chosen to face backward when it is essential that we face forward.

The skills needed now are not routine. Our economy will be increasingly dependent on people who have a good intuitive grasp of the ways in which all kinds of physical and social systems work. They must possess a feeling for mathematical concepts and the ways in which they can be applied to difficult problems, an ability to see patterns of meaning where others see only confusion; a cultivated creativity that leads them to new problems, new products, and new services before their competitors get to them; and, in many cases, the ability to work with other people in complex organizational environments where work groups must decide for themselves how to get the job done.[1]

Current assessment programs are inadequate. New measurement practices must be developed which encompass an expanded range of educational outcomes. Of particular importance is the need for consensus on a set of core curriculum performance indicators for the middle grades. The State Department of Education should provide direct guidance to local districts relative to the use of both traditional and non-traditional assessment practices applicable to core curriculum learning outcomes which are not measured by current standardized tests. This effort should be complemented by the work of local district evaluation departments.

Reliance solely on *quantitative* measurements of learning outcomes is questionable. Standardized test scores may distort assessment of critical middle grade educational reform goals. Some researchers argue persuasively for inclusion of *artistic* judgments as a complement to traditional evaluation measures. This logic is compelling, for example, when considering assessment of complex thinking skills. It is also relevant in considering other types of knowledge and skills which students will require in order to become productive, effective citizens in the world of the 21st century:

Such people will have the need and the ability to learn all the time, as the knowledge required to do their work twists and turns with new challenges and the progress of science and technology. They will not come to the workplace knowing all they have to know, but knowing how to figure out what they need to know, where to get it, and how to make meaning out of it. Even more important, if this country is to remain true to itself, our children should grow up to be humane and caring people, imbued with a set of values that enables them to use their skills in the service of the highest goals of the larger society.[2]

This report includes specific recommendations related to cultural literacy, critical thinking skills, character development, human relationships, emotional and social maturity, personal commitment, and other similarly complex learning outcomes. These echo the Carnegie scenario just cited. They demand not only new instructional goals and strategies but also new means of assessment.

The previous discussion has stressed *student* assessment. *Program* assessment is equally critical. By definition, individual student achievement will falter or flourish based on the relative strength of curricular and instructional programs and the quality of student support services. However, program assessment must be uncoupled from student assessment. There cannot be a reliance on student achievement (CTBS, CAP, etc.) as the only basis for judging program effectiveness. This diminishes the capacity of the entire school community – students, parents, teachers, administrators, and

1 *A Nation Prepared: Teachers for the 21st Century.* Washington, D.C.: Carnegie Forum on Education and the Economy, ©1986, pp. 15, 20. This report was prepared by the Carnegie Forum on Education and the Economy's Task Force on Teaching as a Profession. The Carnegie Forum is a program of the Carnegie Corporation of New York.

2 Ibid., p. 20.

Index of Conditions for Teaching and Learning

Parents usually only see reports on their schools' outputs: test scores and standings in comparison with other schools; course requirements; dropout rates. They also need to see reports on their schools' inputs, so there can be a greater public awareness of the challenges to be met by the community, and the problems that wait down the road if corrective measures are not taken.

Most consumer goods today contain lists of ingredients on their labels, and truth-in-advertising statutes require warnings to the public about many products. The public is entitled to the same information about ingredients affecting its schools.

The State Department of Education should initiate development of an "Index of Conditions for Teaching and Learning" by a task force of teachers, administrators, and research specialists, that must be used by all districts to provide the public with information on every school in a uniform, easy-to-understand format.

The purpose and structure of the index would be based on similar tools used in private industry by such firms as Hewlett-Packard and International Business Machines for monitoring management and productivity of various divisions within the company.

The index should report on at least the following factors:

- Class size and teaching loads.

- Teacher assignments outside area of competence.

- Time spent by teachers on nonteaching tasks.

- Sufficiency and currency of textbooks and teaching materials.

- Availability of qualified personnel to provide counseling and other special services for students.

- Availability of well qualified, adequately compensated substitute teachers.

- Safety, cleanliness, and adequacy of school facilities.

- School order, climate for learning, and behavior problems.

- Adequacy of teacher evaluation and opportunities for professional improvement.

- Teachers' assessment of the quality of school leadership.

Who Will Teach Our Children? A Strategy for Improving California's Schools. Sacramento: The California Commission on the Teaching Profession, 1985, p. 29.

school boards – to take a wider view of the complex, multiple factors which influence individual achievement, schoolwide academic performance, and the efficacy of student support services.

However, when these latter influences are independently evaluated and added to the results of standardized tests, the basis exists for a comprehensive analysis of a school's overall performance. Data are then available which allow for rational decisions relative to program planning and the allocation or reallocation of critical resources.

The recommendation of the California Commission on the Teaching Profession ("Commons Report"- see box), which calls for public reports on both the "outputs" and "inputs" experienced by individual schools, should be implemented in the interests of more valid and comprehensive educational assessment practices.

The list of "input" factors should be expanded to include the following variables:

- Group statistics which describe the character of a student body in terms of influences which impact learning in both positive and negative ways

- Financial resources

- Paraprofessional support

- Parent involvement

- Community support

- School organization

- Instructional philosophy

The State Board of Education should adopt the principles which are presented at the beginning of each section in this report. These should become the basis for defining middle grade program quality criteria for use by local districts in assessing the scope, strength, and efficacy of middle grade educational reform efforts. The evaluation of these efforts must be accompanied by the use of both conventional and newly defined measurement practices.

TASK FORCE RECOMMENDATIONS

❶ The State Department of Education should extend the range of instructional outcomes measured by the CAP (California Assessment Program) tests to include core curriculum performance indicators for the middle grades; CAP testing should occur in the fifth and eighth grades; this change allows conformity with K–5 and 6–8 grade configurations.

❷ The State Department of Education should provide guidance to local districts in the development and use of nontraditional assessment practices designed to evaluate middle grade learning outcomes. Efforts of the State Department of Education to develop non-traditional assessment instruments should be complemented by the work of local district/county evaluation departments.

❸ Local school boards should distinguish between the evaluation of student achievement, as measured by standardized tests, and assessment of instructional programs which include a much broader range of variables; program assessment should be uncoupled from student achievement tests in favor of newer, more comprehensive assessment methodologies.

Continued on next page

RECOMMENDATIONS *Continued*

④ **Local school boards should provide "input" –"output" reports to their communities based on the recommendations of the California Commission on the Teaching Profession; in addition, these reports should contain information related to:**

   a. Statistics which describe the character of student bodies in terms of influences which affect learning in both positive and negative ways

   b. Financial resources

   c. Paraprofessional support

   d. Parent involvement

   e. Community support

   f. School organization

   g. Instructional philosophy

⑤ **Local school boards, administrators, and teachers should compile and utilize assessment data for the primary purpose of program improvement in the areas of curriculum, instruction, and student support services.**

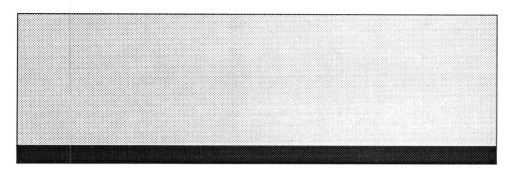

PART FOUR

TEACHING AND ADMINISTRATION:
Preparing for Exemplary Performance

19 Professional Preparation

Middle grade teachers and principals should be prepared to teach/administer grades 6, 7, and 8; specialized preparation should address the content areas of the core curriculum, instructional strategies which emphasize active learning, and the developmental characteristics of young adolescents.

1 John E. Roueche and George A. Baker, III, *Profiling Excellence in America's Schools*. Arlington, Vir.: American Association of School Administrators, ©1986, pp. 87-133.

The professional preparation of middle grade teachers should include specialized knowledge of the core curriculum, the acquisition of a broad repertoire of instructional strategies which relate to active learning and a comprehensive knowledge of the developmental characteristics of young adolescents.

It is urgent that middle grade students experience exemplary teaching. The American Association of School Administrators (AASA), in its recent publication, *Profiling Excellence in America's Schools*,[1] provides a comprehensive analysis of the qualities which most frequently accompany exemplary teaching (see box). In essence, exemplary teachers are highly motivated, are skilled in interpersonal relationships, know their subject matter, and have a broad repertoire of effective instructional strategies which deeply involve them with *every* student, irrespective of individual differences.

The research just cited used the best seller, *In Search of Excellence*, as the basis for studying 154 schools previously identified by the U.S. Department of Education as "The best in America." The authors, in commenting about the findings of their research, emphasize an underlying theme which is pervasive wherever exemplary teaching is present. They characterize this factor as "human skills," which include the involvement of teachers in effective management practices and leadership roles.

The Qualities of Exemplary Teachers

Motivation: The teachers have a strong *commitment to their work and to their students.* "These teachers not only demand achievement, but they provide opportunities for it. ... They select appropriate materials, teach the material thoroughly, monitor frequently, provide much feedback to each student, reteach if necessary, and are especially careful to ensure student success on new material or individual work." They express expectations verbally and clearly.

The teachers are *committed to students outside of class.* Not only do they get involved in students' activities, but they "sacrifice their personal time in order to be accessible to their students who need more guided instruction."

The teachers establish *personal goals* and determine a course of action for attaining them. They hold role models to be very important to them.

The teachers have what the researchers call an *"integrated perception"* of students – they view them as "whole individuals operating in a broader context beyond the classroom."

Also, the teachers stay professionally enthusiastic through a *"reward orientation."* They are rewarded when students exhibit understanding and achieve their goals. "It appears," say the researchers, "that great teaching is inspired by the simple, yet beautiful act of one human being touching another through the learning process."

Interpersonal Skills: The teachers' routines are *carefully patterned* to prevent disruptions; they have a variety of "preventive maintenance" behaviors. The researchers noticed "with-itness," or constant awareness of what was going on in the classroom; and "overlappingness," the ability to do more than one thing at a time. When disruptions do occur, "these teachers approach the problem objectively and methodically."

Continued on next page

They stress that the human skills which make good teachers are often overlooked in the rush to reform America's public schools and that there is not enough preparation of teachers in management skills and leadership skills. The authors believe that these are the qualities that almost all of the reform efforts are ignoring: "If you can start with good human skills you're light years down the road," they conclude.

These skills are particularly important in the middle grades. Young adolescents need teachers who are well organized and who know how to manage an active learning environment with its multiple instructional demands. Students want teachers who give leadership and who enjoy their function as role models, advisers, and mentors. They want and need warm, caring relationships with their teachers. These bonds of understanding and friendship have special significance during the critical, formative middle grade years.

The predominant emphasis in current teacher and administrator professional preparation for the middle grades does not square with either the research findings related to the general qualities associated with teacher and administrator excellence or the particularized educational needs of young adolescents. This imbalance must be redressed if renewal and reform are to occur in middle grade education.

Based on the growing body of research related to teaching excellence and the equally compelling

Continued from previous page

The teachers are *"active listeners"*. The most common technique is paraphrasing, restating students' responses with phrases like "Are you saying that ...?" The teachers also "listen" on paper, sensitive to nuances in students' writing. And they are sensitive to the mood of a class or individual.

Teachers build *rapport* with students by showing them respect, treating them fairly, and trusting them. They show *empathy* by being able to "perceive the thoughts and emotions of their young, teenage students...." They are warm and caring and set high expectations "by laying well-planned paths to success for their students."

Cognitive Skills: The teachers have *individualized perceptions* of their students. They try to find out about them as individuals, "diagnose their needs and learning styles, and then incorporate that knowledge into planned instructional activities." The *effective teaching strategies* used by the teachers include skillful and enthusiastic teaching; well-organized courses; student-centered style; careful monitoring and evaluating; a structured, yet flexible, approach; and active involvement of students. The teachers are deeply involved with their classes. To win over students, good teachers use a combination of techniques, and for them, "no two days are alike."

Having *knowledge* of a subject area and teaching techniques is basic, but the exemplary teachers, "continually engage in professional development, thus presenting and considering themselves as lifelong learners who value the learning process itself." They discuss their "perpetual renewal of knowledge" with enthusiasm.

The teachers actively *seek innovation*. "Our teachers talk animatedly about change to improve students' learning and about taking risks in an attempt to find and adopt new approaches to enhance teaching effectiveness," according to the researchers. In addition, the teachers "take time to reflect on the changes they propose and avoid change for the sake of change."
These findings convey a significant set of expectations for the professional preparation of teachers – expectations that are poorly articulated in too many teacher preparation programs.

John E. Roueche and George A. Baker, III, *Profiling Excellence in America's Schools.* Arlington, Vir.: American Association of School Administrators, ©1986, pp. 87-133.

findings which underlie the necessary conditions for exemplary middle grade education, it is essential that the preparation of middle grade teachers include specialized professional concentration.

Middle grade teachers should receive:

- **Preparation which focuses on the developmental characteristics of early adolescence and the professional skills required to plan and implement successful educational programs for middle grade students.**

Concepts which should receive special attention in the preparation of middle grade teachers include those related to the intellectual, psychological, social, and physical development of young adolescents; and "human skills," including those which relate to group dynamics, principles of motivation, the sociology of change, systems of reward and affirmation, group cohesion, collaborative planning, the dynamics of innovation, multicultural and linguistic influences, conflict resolution, and peer group relationships.

Teachers should develop a broad repertoire of strategies related to the management of complex human relationships appropriate to their work with young adolescents. Special emphases should be given to the development of knowledge and skills essential for teacher leadership roles in adviser-advisee programs and group guidance activities of various kinds.

- **Preparation in pedagogical studies specifically related to middle grade curriculum and instructional issues.**

Major emphasis should be given to the mastery of a repertoire of instructional strategies which involve active learning on the part of all students. The middle grade core curriculum should receive special attention, with particular focus given to the study of issues and recommendations found elsewhere in this report.

Teachers should demonstrate proficiency in the use of cooperative learning techniques and be able to recognize and respond to individual learning difficulties.

The emerging capacity of middle grade students to use higher-order cognitive skills should be thoroughly understood. Implications for instructional strategies in specific subjects should be understood at a practical level of implementation.

Teachers must have the capability to teach reading and writing skills as a logical extension of their specialist or generalist teaching assignments. The philosophy of a schoolwide reading and writing program throughout the middle grades should become a professonal commitment that is translated into daily instructional activities at the classroom level.

The tension between intellectual and academic priorities and the emotional and social dimensions of adolescence should be thoroughly explored. Teachers must emerge from their pedagogical studies with a clear sense of the middle grade philosophy and a strong commitment to its principles.

There are significant additional recommendations which must accompany improved teacher preparation:

- **Principal endorsement.**

A need exists to strengthen the preparation of principals assigned to the middle grades. Their academic emphasis should include the same priorities as defined for teachers but with additional stress on planning, organizing, implementing (including master scheduling), and evaluating middle grade educational programs.

- **Reassignment of teachers and principals from K–5 or 9–12 to middle grade instruction.**

The reassignment of teachers and principals to grades 6, 7, and 8 from either grades K–5 or 9–12 should occur on the basis of interest, expertise, and commitment. Middle grade professionals should understand and enjoy young adolescents. Their training should specifically prepare them for this level of education. Those who are reassigned should either demonstrate or acquire the specialized training described above. Assistance in paying for the tuition of reassigned personnel by local districts is strongly encouraged.

- **Undergraduate field experience.**

Early field experiences should be provided for undergraduate students considering middle grade teaching as a career option. This should be a focused, supervised experience which develops awareness of middle grade educational philosophy, knowledge of students' characteristics, and a generalized sense of school organization and curriculum and instructional practices.

Participation in student advisement programs and one-to-one tutoring are encouraged as methods for giving undergraduate students direct contact with young adolescents. Similar field experiences should be made available to those who already hold the baccalaureate degree and who are considering a career reorientation or a major career change from another professional field.

- **Underrepresented minority teachers.**

Deliberate attempts should be made to recruit underrepresented minorities to the teaching profession. New and innovative strategies

---

Effective Principals

Effective principals have a vision of what a good school is and systematically strive to bring that vision to life in their schools. School improvement is their constant theme. They scrutinize existing practices to assure that all activities and procedures contribute to the quality of the time available for learning. They make sure teachers participate actively in this process. Effective principals, for example, make opportunities available for faculty to improve teaching and classroom management skills.

Good school leaders protect the school day for teaching and learning. They do this by keeping teachers' administrative chores and classroom interruptions to a minimum.

Effective principals visibly and actively support learning. Their practices create an orderly environment. Good principals make sure teachers have the necessary materials and the kind of assistance they need to teach well.

Effective principals also build morale in their teachers. They help teachers create a climate of achievement by encouraging new ideas; they also encourage teachers to help formulate school teaching policies and select textbooks. They try to develop community support for the school, its faculty, and its goals.

What Works: Research about Teaching and Learning. Prepared under the direction of William J. Bennett. Washington, D.C.: United States Department of Education, 1986, p. 50.

must be developed for achieving this goal. These should be implemented as early as the middle grades. (See section on Student Diversity and Underrepresented Minorities.)

- **Team and collaborative teaching.**

Instructional strategies appropriate for the middle grades, such as team and collaborative teaching, are presently difficult to implement legally because of existing credentialing restrictions. The elementary (K-8) certificate is valid for teachers assigned to self-contained classrooms. The secondary (7-12) certificate is valid only for the subject(s) specified on the credential. In order to legally implement a humanities core curriculum block involving two or more discrete subjects, substantive changes must be made in existing regulations affecting teaching assignments in grades 6, 7, and 8.

The Commission on Teacher Credentialing must revise and clarify its certification regulations in order to permit greater flexibility and innovation in the design of middle grade instructional strategies. This is a matter of the highest priority.

- **Collaboration between institutions of higher education and the State Department of Education.**

There should be immediate initiatives designed to facilitate collaboration among institutions of higher education, the Commission on Teacher Credentialing, and the State Department of Education for the purpose of planning and implementing the steps required to strengthen the professional preparation of educators assigned to the middle grades.

TASK FORCE RECOMMENDATIONS

❶ The Commission on Teacher Credentialing (CTC) and institutions of higher education (IHE) which provide teacher/administrator preparation programs should ensure that candidates for K–8 and 7–12 teaching and administrative credentials are more effectively prepared for assignments to grades 6, 7, and 8. The CTC and IHE's should incorporate the following emphases in teacher and administration credentialing programs:

a. Developmental characteristics of early adolescence; "human skills" essential for planning effective teacher/counselor/ principal interaction with young adolescents; teaching strategies appropriate to "active learning"; and comprehensive understanding of the philosophy of the middle grade core curriculum.

b. In addition to the emphases defined above, principals should receive special preparation related to planning, organizing, implementing (including the theory and development of scheduling strategies), and evaluating middle grade educational programs.

❷ Local school boards should amend personnel policies in order to give preference in the assignment of teachers and principals to grades 6, 7, and 8 based on those who have received special emphasis in their professional preparation relative to middle grade education.

❸ Superintendents should initiate local district cooperation with institutions of higher education in order to provide teachers, counselors, and principals presently assigned

Continued on next page

RECOMMENDATIONS *Continued*

to grades 6, 7, and 8 with staff development opportunities that enable them to acquire specialized knowledge and skills in the areas defined in recommendations 1a and 1b, above.

❹ Institutions of higher education should provide early field experience options for undergraduate students who have potential interest in middle grade education.

❺ Institutions of higher education should more intensively recruit underrepresented minority students to the teaching profession. New and innovative efforts should occur, including attractive financial aid options for those who pursue professional training to the level of certification. The identification of potential minority teachers should begin as early as the middle grades. (See chapter on Student Diversity and Underrepresented Minorities.)

❻ The Commission on Teacher Credentialing should revise requirements related to K–8 and 7–12 credentials in order to allow local districts to assign either elementary or secondary teachers to humanities core blocks (or similar interdisciplinary configurations) in the middle grades.

❼ Local boards of education should ensure balance and reasonableness in the assignments of middle grade teachers. The numbers of assigned students and subject-matter preparations should be weighed in relation to the responsibilities of teachers for direct involvement in guidance activities, extracurricular and intramural programs, and other specialized support services inherent in middle grade reform efforts. Teaching loads should be limited in terms of the numbers of assigned students and subject-matter preparations.

20 Staff Development

Middle grade teachers and principals should participate in comprehensive, well-planned, long-range staff development programs which emphasize professional collegiality.

Staff development priorities should have their antecedents in the philosophy of the core curriculum, the qualities of teaching excellence, and the characteristics of young adolescents. These categories of educational concern related to the middle grades have equal significance for those enrolled in professional preparation programs and those who are already experienced teachers, counselors, and principals. There is an important difference, however. Pre-service professional preparation must be more generic in its orientation, even when partially field-based. Long-range planning in relation to a given school, its students, and one's colleagues is impossible.

This is not the case when one receives a permanent professional appointment. The potential then exists for a collegial relationship which enables a professional staff to focus on a particular school, its program, its students, and families. Patterns of cooperative, collaborative staff relationships can be developed which enable productive long-range educational planning to occur.

Teachers must have the major role in defining the content, design, and implementation of school-based staff development activities. These may take many forms limited only by the creativity of those who provide leadership to others or who

take responsibility for their own developmental needs.

Formal and informal settings can contribute equally to the achievement of staff development goals. As an example, Lipsitz notes:

"The common planning period [for multidisciplinary teams] also promotes collegiality and professionalism in curriculum development and review."[1]

The same theme is picked up in the Carnegie Report:

Fundamental to our conception of a workable professional environment that fosters learning is more time for all professional teachers to reflect, plan, and discuss teaching innovations and problems with their colleagues.[2]

In essence, staff development programs represent the substance of a long-range professional commitment to continue to grow intellectually, to gain new skills, and to refine the quality of one's performance and to do so in a rational

1 Published by permission of Transaction, Inc., *Successful Schools for Young Adolescents*, by Joan Lipsitz. ©1984 by Transaction, Inc., p. 194.

2 *A Nation Prepared: Teachers for the 21st Century*. Washington, D.C.: Carnegie Forum on Education and the Economy, ©1986, p. 60. This report was prepared by the Carnegie Forum on Education and the Economy's Task Force on Teaching as a Profession. The Carnegie Forum is a program of the Carnegie Corporation of New York.

Reframing

… the students we need to develop can be reframed to describe the kinds of teachers needed to support the learning of those students. Teachers should have a good grasp of the ways in which all kinds of physical and social systems work; a feeling for what data are and the uses to which they can be put; an ability to help students see patterns of meaning where others see only confusion; an ability to foster genuine creativity in students; and the ability to work with other people in work groups that decide for themselves how to get the job done.

A Nation Prepared: Teachers for the 2lst Century. Washington, D.C.: Carnegie Forum on Education and the Economy, ©1986, p. 25. This report was prepared by the Carnegie Forum on Education and the Economy's Task Force on Teaching as a Profession. The Carnegie Forum is a program of the Carnegie Corporation of New York.

way. Certain staff development goals are intrinsic to the needs of individual teachers. Others are intrinsic to the needs of their school, their department, their team, or their grade level. Still other goals may be defined in terms of district-level priorities. Accountability for planning and implementing staff development activities shifts in relation to the source of the priority.

A portion of staff development time should address priorities set by individuals; a portion should address school, grade-level, or departmental priorities set by groups of teachers and school administrators; and a portion should address district priorities set by the school boards and the superintendents.

The alignment of staff development objectives with curriculum and instructional goals should be formally supported by changes in school and district personnel, leadership, and fiscal practices. Districts should be responsible for the basic instructional materials which teachers require to implement what they have been trained to do, especially in relation to district and school priorities.

Teachers, counselors, principals, and central office personnel are mutually accountable for achieving the alignment of staff development objectives. Priorities should be clearly defined at each level of decision making. If logical interrelationships are absent, then they should be addressed and resolved.

Middle grade professionals face an especially challenging set of responsibilities. The level of complexity found in the developmental characteristics of young adolescents represents one of the most intense periods of change in the lives of human beings, rivaled only by the experiences of infancy. Teachers must factor this transition into the instructional equation. They are

Teacher Support Groups

No program can be transplanted into your classroom exactly as it was designed. As the Rand Change Agent Study (Berman and McLaughlin, 1978) noted, successful change in schools is an "adaptive" and "heuristic" process. This means that programs designed for one setting need to be modified to fit the constraints of a different workplace. It also means that teachers and administrators must work at making a program meet their own needs by finding varied ways to meet program objectives.

One way to do this is to establish peer support groups for coaching and problem-posing and resolving. These groups could be in the form of seminars, additional workshops, and informal meetings before, during, and after school. Such a peer strategy is essential to the success of any change program and especially for those that involve such complex role reorientation as programs to foster thinking. ...

Support groups foster intellectual growth for teachers by providing a secure environment where problems may be presented and rational problem-solving processes [are] used to best advantage. They also help teachers encounter the realities of challenging students to transcend the hidden curriculum and their own cognitive developmental stages. ...

Problem-posing and problem-resolving support groups need to be built into the staff development process from the very beginning. These groups may be led by teachers, staff developers, consultants, or supervisors. Persons conducting seminars should possess ... openness, trust, willingness to confront difficulties, [and should search] for causes and the universe of alternative solutions. They must exemplify trust, good communications processes, and, above all, be removed from the evaluative process. Teachers must be able to confront their own strengths and weaknesses in an atmosphere free from the fear or threat of subsequent evaluation.

John Barell, "Removing Impediments to Change," in *Developing Minds: A Resource Book for Teaching Thinking*. Edited by Arthur L. Costa. Alexandria, Vir.: Association for Supervision and Curriculum Development, ©1985, p. 36. Reprinted with permission of the Association for Supervision and Curriculum Development. All rights reserved.

expected to do so, without compromising the integrity of the curriculum and without any diminishing of student achievement as measured by standardized tests.

Because teachers carry an enormous responsibility when their jobs are done well, it is easy for them to become disenchanted in the midst of multiple educational reform efforts and for staff development efforts to become blurred – even fragmented. The Carnegie Report captures the essence of this concern:

... Many of the best people now staffing our schools, people who meet the requirements we have just laid out, are immensely frustrated – to the point of cynicism.

They see little change in the things that matter most to them, few policy developments that would enable them to meet the needs that have been described. They see the bureaucratic structure within which they work becoming even more rigid, and the opportunities for exercising professional judgment becoming even more limited. Increasingly, they believe that teachers are being made to pay the price for reform, and many do not believe that the current conception of reform will lead to real gains for students.

Reasonable people can differ as to the merits of these charges, but it is certainly true that real reform cannot be accomplished despite teachers. It will only come with their active participation. There is a real danger now of political gridlock, a situation in which those who would improve the schools from the outside are met by teachers on the inside who, because they distrust policy makers' motives and disapprove of their methods, will prevent further progress.[3]

The anxiety reflected in these comments need not occur in relation to middle grade renewal in California. Effective, professionally oriented staff development programs represent a central step in making certain that reform efforts which directly involve teachers, counselors, and principals are planned and implemented in an orderly manner.

Much can be achieved through staff development activities at the levels of individual, group, school, and district program planning. There are three fundamental themes around which the majority of middle grade staff development activity should be organized:

- Academic content (growth in knowledge and skills related to the disciplines which one is assigned to teach – particularly in the core curriculum)

- Human skills (growth in knowledge and skills related to human interaction among young adolescents and between members of the professional staff and students)

- Pedagogical theory and practice (growth in knowledge and skills related to instructional practices appropriate to the developmental characteristics of young adolescents and consistent with the thrust of the core curriculum frameworks)

Staff development activities which are planned by individuals, faculty committees, teaching teams, principals, counseling and guidance specialists, central office administrators and other significant professional and paraprofessional personnel must complement each other.

3 *A Nation Prepared: Teachers for the 21st Century.* Washington, D.C.: Carnegie Forum on Education and the Economy, ©1986, p. 26. This report was prepared by the Carnegie Forum on Education and the Economy's Task Force on Teaching as a Profession. The Carnegie Forum is a program of the Carnegie Corporation of New York.

But . . . Do I Have the Time to Do It Right?

Teachers should ask themselves, "Have my students really been learning what I have been teaching them, and can they put that knowledge to work in creative and critical thinking situations?" When I asked myself that question, the answer was, "No, my students have short-term memories; what they seem to learn one week is gone the next."... It does not matter how much material you cover; if the students don't understand it and can't use it when you are finished teaching, it is useless to them.

If you want to change your students' attitudes toward learning, you should have them listen to each other and give them time to think before speaking. You should design your lessons around the basic questioning format that requires students to gather facts and process them using higher cognitive skills. I am convinced that good questioning skills improve student learning, and I have been trying to pass this notion on to other teachers.

The question that comes up at almost every workshop I conduct is, "But ... it sounds like it takes too much time. I have to get through the book or my curriculum, and how will I be able to do that if I spend so much time questioning?" Since I have changed my method of questioning students, I have found that my students have changed their attitudes toward learning. This change, very subtle at first, is now quite startling. They pay attention; they listen to each other and give answers that show they are thinking about what they are going to say. I find that the quality of their questions has also improved; they seem to have a better understanding of the concepts and are showing improvement on tests and written work. Since I have become used to this new style, the amount of material I cover seems to be about the same now as it was in the past, although I must admit that, when I was learning to use good questioning techniques, the process did take longer.

The other question that I commonly hear is, "Do I have to change my teaching strategies?" Of course not! All teaching strategies require teachers to ask questions and students to answer them. The only thing you will change is your style of questioning, and that alone will allow your students to take a quantum jump in their ability to learn the material presented and truly understand how to apply it to problem-solving situations.

Let's face it – education has been under fire for some time, and we need to do all we can to improve our product. Our product is educated students, and through the implementation of sound questioning practices we can improve the quality of student education without the addition of a single dollar to our budgets or an extra minute to our teaching day.

Dave Schumaker, "But...Do I Have the Time to Do It Right?" in *Developing Minds: A Resource Book for Teaching Thinking.* Edited by Arthur L. Costa. Alexandria, Vir.: Association for Supervision and Curriculum Development, ©1985, p. 130. Reprinted with permission of the Association for Supervision and Curriculum Development. All rights reserved.

Allocations of time, materials, budgets, and other resources must be tested at every level of decision making for their contribution to the realization of goals related to the themes of middle grade educational reform. School-based and district-level planning committees can help to ensure that this occurs.

Among specific staff development possibilities which these themes suggest are: defining school philosophy; planning the curriculum; learning about adolescent characteristics; studying the dynamics of interdisciplinary teaming; setting up adviser-advisee programs; reviewing advances in the core curriculum subjects; developing deeper understanding of learning styles; mastering the varied forms of cooperative teaching; learning group dynamics skills; studying motivational strategies; planning and implementing individual or group innovations in varied areas of professional practice; developing collaborative teaching styles; maintaining discipline; designing active learning environments; and evaluating the outcomes of programs and projects.

Boards must allocate resources to facilitate multiple forms of staff development. Superintendents and principals should identify creative alternatives for scheduling allocations of time required to implement varied types of staff development programs. Teachers, principals, and superintendents should collaboratively plan to ensure balance among individual, school, and district-level staff development priorities.

Systematic, long-range staff development goals should be set by each professional. Groups of professionals should be bound together by common roles and shared assignments characterized by an integrated and focused response to the broad themes of middle grade reform and renewal.

Highlights from Research on Staff Development for Effective Teaching

Studies comparing various models or processes of staff development are rare. While it is not possible to state conclusively that one in-service design is superior to another, we can put together the many pieces of research reviewed here to make some general recommendations about staff development programs for more effective teaching.

1. Select content that has been verified by research to improve student achievement.
2. Create a context of acceptance by involving teachers in decision making and providing both logistical and psychological administrative support.
3. Conduct training sessions (more than one) two or three weeks apart.
4. Include presentation, demonstration, practice, and feedback as workshop activities.
5. Provide opportunities for small-group discussions of the application of new practices and sharing of ideas and concerns about effective instruction during training sessions.
6. Encourage teachers between workshops to visit each others' classrooms, preferably with a simple, objective, student-centered observation instrument. Provide opportunities for discussions of the observation.
7. Develop in teachers a philosophical acceptance of the new practices by presenting research and a rationale for the effectiveness of the techniques. Allow teachers to express doubts about or objections to the recommended methods in the small group. Let the other teachers convince the resisting teacher of the usefulness of the practices through "testimonies" of their use and effectiveness.
8. Lower teachers' perception of the cost of adopting a new practice through detailed discussions of the "nuts and bolts" of using the technique and teacher sharing of experiences with the technique.
9. Help teachers grow in their self-confidence and competence through encouraging them to try only one or two new practices after each workshop. Diagnosis of teacher strengths and weaknesses can help the trainer suggest changes that are likely to be successful – and, thus, reinforce future efforts to change.
10. Plan to take more time for teaching practices that require very complex thinking skills, provide more practice, and consider activities that develop conceptual flexibility.

Georgea M. Sparks, "Synthesis of Research on Staff Development for Effective Teaching," *Educational Leadership*, Vol. 41 (November, 1983), pp. 65-72. Reprinted with permission of the Association for Supervision and Curriculum Development. ©1986 by the Association for Supervision and Curriculum Development. All rights reserved.

TASK FORCE RECOMMENDATIONS

❶ The state Legislature should provide financial incentives to local districts to be used for middle grade staff development programs which focus on:

a. Increased mastery of academic content

b. Increased knowledge of the characteristics of young adolescents and the critical repertoire of human skills required for effective teaching, counseling; and mentoring of students at this age level

c. Increased levels of knowledge and skill derived from pedagogical studies – particularly those which lead to a broad base of instructional strategies which emphasize active learning and which are responsive to the multiple individual differences of young adolescents

❷ Superintendents should facilitate the planning of comprehensive, long-range staff development programs for the middle grades to include:

a. Collaborative planning among teachers, counselors, principals, and central office personnel

b. Guarantees of balance among individual, school-level, and district-level staff development priorities

c. Provision for multiple types of staff development programs, including those which have the potential for long-term professional growth

d. Assurances of systematically planned, goal-oriented programs which allow substantive middle grade reform efforts to be achieved

Continued on next page

RECOMMENDATIONS *Continued*

③ Superintendents should support efforts of teaching principals and faculties to implement middle grade curriculum and instructional improvements.

This support should include:

a. Understanding of what is being attempted by principals and faculties in sufficient detail to:

- **Recognize and encourage progress, even when imperfect.**

- **Enlist the support of parents and the community for program improvements.**

- **Overcome obstacles and solve problems that inevitably accompany change.**

b. Creating a districtwide culture, through example and encouragement, which provides a joyful response to progress in implementing school-based improvements and a good-humored attitude toward mistakes and frustrations which occur in the process.

c. Marshaling resources to support individual school improvements.

d. Revising district-level policies and administrative practices, where required, in order to support the implementation of innovative practices at the local school level.

④ Superintendents, central office administrators, and principals should provide collaborative leadership in solving logistical problems. Such leadership is essential to the successful

Continued on next page

RECOMMENDATIONS *Continued*

implementation of comprehensive staff
development programs, including:

a. Provision of adequate blocks of time for
   professional learning activities

b. Allocation of convenient sites and
   appropriate facilities

c. Provision of materials, equipment, and
   other resources, as needed, to allow
   mastery of staff development goals

d. Provision of quality controls and general
   program evaluation which guide long-
   range efforts to attain major reform goals

PART FIVE

LEADERSHIP AND PARTNERSHIP:

Defining the Catalysts for
Middle Grade Educational Reform

21 Parents, Communities, and School Boards

Parents, communities, and school boards should share accountability for middle grade educational reform.

Parents, community members, and their elected representatives who make up the membership of local school boards constitute the keystone of any educational reform effort. Their respective roles are critical to any consideration of substantive change. Without their collective support any discussion of innovation and renewal is trivial-

ized. The roles of parents, community members, and local school boards in middle grade school reform efforts must be viewed along a continuum of leadership rather than as separate efforts which intersect in an unplanned and random fashion.

Parents represent the single most important citizen group in terms of school support. If parents sustain the importance of a particular innovation or practice, the result is catalytic in terms of generating community and board support. The opposite is also true. Parental perceptions of school reform efforts can differ markedly from those of the professional staff with respect to relative priorities.

Goodlad offers valuable insights about differences between parent and teacher perceptions:

At both junior and senior high school levels, there is an interesting slant to the data once we look beyond student misbehavior and drugs/alcohol as problems on which there is rather close agreement among teachers, parents, and students. ... This slant is accentuated when we look at [teachers'] responses to the question, "What is this school's one biggest problem?" The most frequent choice was "lack of student interest." Our parents' top problems [were] student misbehavior and drugs and alcohol. ... But other data point to parents' concern also about whether their children were nurtured as individuals in the school setting. ... slightly more than half of junior and senior high parents disagreed with the statement, "My child receives a lot of individual attention from his/her teacher." Approximately the same number of parents agreed with

---

Guidelines for Collaborative Work: School and Community Leaders Working Together

These guidelines suggest how we can take collective responsibility for improving schools. The climate for reform gives us a rare opportunity to change the ways we work that may be both deep and lasting.

* Some type of organizational structure is needed to collaborate.
* A small core of people actually work on the collaboration.
* Time for collaboration needs to be allotted.
* Skillful people working together enhance collaborative work.
* Initially, *activities* propel the collaboration, not goals.
* Large superordinate goals for collaboration become clearer after people have worked together.
* People often underestimate the amount of energy it takes to work with other people.
* Collaboration with schools demands an understanding of schools as complex social organizations shaped by the realities of specific contexts.
* Ambiguity and flexibility more aptly describe collaborations than certainty and rigidity.
* Conflict in collaborative work is inevitable; it has the potential for productive learning.
* People can participate in collaborative work for different reasons, but they should include wanting to do things together.
* Products created by collaborating create an important sense of pride in collaborative work.
* Shared experiences over time build mutual trust, respect, risk-taking, and commitment.

Ann Lieberman, "Collaborative Work," *Educational Leadership*, Vol. 43 (February, 1986), p. 7. Reprinted with permission of the Association for Supervision and Curriculum Development. ©1986 by the Association for Supervision and Curriculum Development. All rights reserved.

the statement, *"Average students don't get enough attention at this school."*

Our data further suggest mounting concern on the part of parents over the attention given their children as these students advanced upward through the grades. Students, much like parents, reflected a greater concern than teachers over non academic problems. ... In seeking to improve our schools, we may discover that some gains in standardized achievement test scores will not satisfy the full array of interests that parents and students have in their schools, interests that reach to the whole of life and extend well beyond academics.[1]

Lipsitz echoes the same theme but suggests that exemplary school practices can reverse parental anxiety and build community support:

Parents are generally very apprehensive about the middle years of schooling. Junior high schools have been seen for many years as the least productive and most worrisome of public educational institutions. ... classes for parents on early adolescent development, aspects of peer relationships, and school life...bind them with loyalty to the school while helping them to understand family interactions and school practices. ... The reports of parents who participate in these school activities help set a tone that fosters school support in the community.[2]

Both Goodlad and Lipsitz signal the importance of a middle grade philosophy that embraces intellectual, emotional, and social priorities. Parents want this balance in the education of their young adolescent children, and they apparently want to be close to the process. The middle grade philosophy reflected in this report has the potential to reverse the trends which Goodlad, Lipsitz, and Epstein identify. A school environment which

---

Home-School Cooperation

Joyce Epstein and other researchers at the Johns Hopkins University Center for Social Organization of Schools involved thousands of teachers in 600 schools and more than 1,200 parents in their study of home and school cooperation. Major findings include:

- Students' reading scores and study habits, in particular, improve when parental help is given at home.

- Relatively few teachers make frequent or systematic use of parent involvement activities.

- Teachers are often "taught" to keep parents out of the learning process.

- There is a dramatic decline of parental involvement as students grow older.

- Many parents lose touch with the school, their children's efforts, and the sequences of their children's decisions about school programs and courses.

James J. Fenwick. *The Middle School Years.* San Diego, Calif.: Fenwick Associates, ©1986, p. 54.

---

honors academic excellence while stressing a pervasive sense of professional concern for each student's physical, emotional, and social needs represents a highly attractive setting which parents not only understand and respect but also one in which they feel both welcome and able to participate.

The ASCD study of 130 exemplary middle schools, cited earlier in this report, found that parental involvement and support were strengthened markedly following reorganization of the middle grades:

Survey respondents proudly described the positive parental involvement and support they experienced after reorganization to middle schools. They cited better attendance at open houses, conferences, and PTA meetings, as well as a greater propensity to volunteer as chaperones for field trips, dances, or other school socials; to help in libraries, cafeterias, and classrooms; to coach intramural athletics; and to teach

1 John I. Goodlad, *A Place Called School.* New York: McGraw Hill Book Company, ©1984, pp. 74-75. Reprinted by permission of the publisher.

2 Published by permission of Transaction, Inc., from *Successful Schools for Young Adolescents,* by Joan Lipsitz. ©1984 by Transaction, Inc., pp. 196-97.

minicourses in many of the exemplary middle schools. Administrators cultivated parental involvement during all stages of the transition, anticipating the potential value of their contributions and support. They took pains to explain why and how reorganization would improve schooling for their children and established communication channels that encouraged parents to ask questions and to make suggestions at any point in the reorganization process.

Administrators sought to capitalize on parental willingness to share responsibility for their children's education and were well rewarded for their efforts. One respondent boasted that parents told him, "You cannot change your program until my last child has gone through it!" and "My child likes school for the first time." Parents often voiced support for the middle school at board meetings and frequently voted to provide the money needed to maintain the level of educational services characteristic of exemplary middle schools.[3]

Community support and, ultimately, board support of educational reform efforts are direct functions of parent support for their schools. Parents shape educational policy either through their involvement or noninvolvement in school affairs. An educational philosophy that embraces parental concerns about their young adolescent children will do much to diminish the present distance between classroom and home and ultimately enable educators to achieve significant professional goals.

Herbert Walberg, research professor at the University of Illinois (Chicago), claims that there is a definite "curriculum of the home" which educators can promote. Stanford professors Patrick Shields and Milbrey McLaughlin assert that active parents can help schools politically. This happens if schools value parent involvement and communities encourage it. These researchers insist that parent involvement is essential but unlikely to occur through mandated policies:

... parents want to help their child's education and the increasing number of non-mainstream children makes it even more imperative for schools to reach out and engage parents. Mandated parent involvement has not been implemented as reformers intended. ... [Another tack should be tried.] This would be to provide incen-

Translating Ideals into Reality

Renewal and reform in the middle grades means that every community from the Siskiyous to the San Ysidro Mountains, from the Pacific to Lake Tahoe must be willing to put its own imprint on new principles of middle grade education. The larger urban districts will do this in a different way than will the smaller districts of the rural north. The medium-sized districts will each have their own unique response. It should not be otherwise. The most significant factor about any major change is that it must be able to be accommodated to the unique interests, ideals, and values of local communities without losing its essential qualities – its integrity. This is the challenge of middle grade educational reform in California.

To speak of academic reform in the middle grades of the state, under these circumstances, is to demand the most critical and innovative thought on the part of those who make or administer educational policy. The leadership of the State Department of Education is especially vital in bringing renewal to the middle grades. It is crucial that the respective roles of the State Board of Education and the State Superintendent of Public Instruction are exercised in galvanizing public support with respect to educational, political, and fiscal issues.

The State Department of Education must also be the catalyst for shaping public opinion in support of a new philosophy of middle grade education. It must define that philosophy in practical, operational terms that cut across demographic, ethnic, linguistic, and geographic barriers that have the potential to break the back of any reform effort, no matter how carefully conceived. It is at this point that the direct support of local school boards, community leaders, and parents must become visible; it is the point at which ideals are translated into reality.

tives ...for teachers and administrators to change their attitude about parent involvement. Educate teachers about the merits of helping parents help their children and educate administrators about the benefits of parent participation. Change of the nature and level required depends on motivating teachers and administrators to try.[4]

Parents and educators who wish to see reforms in middle grade education must start at the level of the local school. There must be cooperation and collaboration in developing a model of education based on both parental and professional priorities. The perceptions of parents that they are unwanted and the perceptions of teachers and principals that parents are uninterested need to be faced and resolved.

When even a small cadre of parents begins to sense a new spirit of openness and deep concern for all dimensions of the lives of their young adolescent children by school personnel, the results can be electric. Other less involved – even uninvolved – parents are quick to pick up the cues. Instead of school-home tensions regarding changes of policy, a strong political base for implementing reform efforts begins to emerge.

Parent leadership can extend this expression of support beyond the school and into the community. Businesses, civic groups, professional organizations, and the political structure of a community are eager to support educational change when they sense strong parental backing.

Boards of education are elected to give leadership in matters of educational policy, finance, and governance. Their willingness to endorse major policy changes related to middle grade organization and educational practices is highly dependent on their ability to measure the levels of parent and community support for their actions. The roles which school board members exercise is critical to middle grade reform efforts. Without this ultimate level of support, there will be no renewal.

Educational change may come from the top down or eventually surface through the creative efforts of individuals who occupy more obscure roles. There will always be tension between those who initiate action and those who must react to it. Superintendents and local school boards should seek in every way possible to help parents, the general public, and the professional staff to interact creatively and constructively regarding proposals for middle grade educational reform, regardless of the direction from which leadership emerges.

At some point, local school boards will respond to the recommendations for middle grade reform and renewal which are presented in this report. Many recommendations call for actions which only they have the power to authorize. They must be willing to confront the fact that education for young adolescents requires specialized curricular, instructional, and organizational support systems without which substantive reform efforts will be impossible to achieve.

4 *Education USA*, Vol. 28 (June 23, 1986), p. 326, ©1986. Reprinted by permission from *Education USA*, National School Public Relations Association.

TASK FORCE RECOMMENDATIONS

❶ The state Superintendent of Public Instruction should recommend adoption of the report of the Middle Grade Task Force to the State Board of Education as the basis of public educational policy for the middle grades.

❷ The Superintendent and the State Board of Education should make specific recommendations to the California Legislature to enable the implementation of the Task Force's recommendations requiring legislative action.

❸ The Superintendent of Public Instruction should initiate appropriate administrative steps within the State Department of Education designed to strengthen and support middle grade education based on specific Task Force recommendations.

❹ School district governing boards and county boards of education should adopt the report of the Middle Grade Task Force as the basis for public and professional forums which address the education of young adolescents. These forums should involve multiple categories of interested citizens, including:

a. Parents and students

b. Community leaders

c. Teachers and administrators

d. Leaders of business and industry

e. Representatives of institutions of higher education

The primary purpose of public and professional forums should be to review and recommend specific action on Task Force

Continued on next page

RECOMMENDATIONS *Continued*

recommendations, with particular emphasis on those which have direct meaning for local districts and/or individual schools.

⑤ Superintendents should propose policy changes to their school boards related to the Task Force's recommendations based on their assessment of responses from public and professional forums and their own convictions regarding middle grade educational reform and renewal.

⑥ School district governing boards and county boards of education should delete, amend, and/or adopt policies designed to strengthen middle grade education based on their own assessment of the Task Force's recommendations, their review of recommendations growing out of public and professional forums, and their analysis of specific policies recommended by their respective superintendents.

⑦ The State Department of Education should develop models of parent involvement which provide varied, explicit strategies for developing cooperative relationships between home and school.

22 State -of -the -Art Middle Grade Schools

A partnership involving local school districts, institutions of higher education, and the State Department of Education should be created to facilitate the development of 100 state-of-the-art middle grade schools; the mission of these schools should be to serve as a catalyst for middle grade educational reform throughout California.

The concept of a network of 100 state-of-the-art middle grade schools represents an exciting and adventurous response to the findings and recommendations of the Middle Grade Task Force. These schools would provide the basis for collaborative and collegial efforts designed to give a cutting edge to middle grade educational reform. They would become centers of program development, drawing teachers, counselors, and principals from throughout California to observe, study, and design programs for implementation in their own districts.

In effect, these state-of-the-art middle schools would subscribe to the following commitments:

- Indicate their willingness to plan and implement new, innovative strategies, programs, practices, and policies which have the potential to facilitate the achievement of middle grade educational reform goals.

- Demonstrate their willingness to engage in research-oriented activities related to instructional issues and to systematically evaluate and report findings through varied forums.

- Make a multiple-year commitment in order to allow the critical steps of planning, implementing, and evaluating (both formative and summative) to occur in relation to program development.

- Demonstrate their willingness to communicate – to create linkages between people and institutions that allow a steady flow of formal and informal ideas and concepts, designed to convey information, to share resources, and to change and improve middle grade education in substantive ways.

- Share their desire to be a catalyst for middle grade educational renewal and reform throughout California; to use the networking capabilities of the partnership to disseminate widely the results of their efforts to all levels of public education.

- Agree to become a "clinical" school and to accept responsibility for training teachers, counselors, principals and others in the areas of curriculum, instruction, organization, counseling, guidance, adolescent development, community involvement, and other areas related to middle grade educational reform.

The Carnegie Report, *A Nation Prepared: Teachers for the 21st Century*, provides an example of a contemporary definition of a clinical school:

> ... *These institutions, having an analogous role to teaching hospitals, should be outstanding public schools working closely with schools of education. ... teachers in these schools should hold adjunct appointments in schools of education. ... The clinical schools should exemplify the collegial, performance-oriented environment that newly certified teachers should be prepared to establish. By connecting elementary and secondary education and higher education in a much more direct way than is typically the case now, these new institutions will create a valuable linkage between the elementary and secondary schools, the schools of education, and the arts and sciences departments.*[1]

Apart from the inclusion of staff and students in a California-wide network of state-of-the-art middle grade schools, the time is right to invite representatives of institutions of higher education with teacher preparation programs to also share in this venture. Readiness for this type of participation is implied in recent public statements by major committees of The California State University (CSU). For example, in its report, *Excellence in Professional Education* (1983), the Advisory Committee to Study Programs in Education in the CSU System urges the Chancellor to establish an advisory committee whose members shall be drawn from key sources, including "... *public school teachers and administrators ... [and] the State Department of Education .... The Advisory Committee shall provide liaison for communication and influence.*[2]

There is every reason to believe that private institutions of higher education are equally ready – even enthusiastic – about participating in a consortium of middle grade schools, colleges, and universities dedicated to middle grade educational reform.

Procedurally, the Superintendent of Public Instruction should identify and invite 100 schools throughout California, from among nominations and applications from local districts, to serve as the nucleus of the network of state-of-the-art middle grade schools. Institutions of higher education, through their schools of education, should be invited and encouraged to apply for participation in this partnership. The final selection of middle grade schools and schools of education should become the respective responsibilities of the Superintendent of Public Instruction and the presidents of participating colleges and universities.

The Superintendent of Public Instruction, the State Board of Education, and the presidents of participating institutions of higher education and their respective boards should request the Legislature, Governor, and private foundations to collaborate in planning, funding, and implementing this partnership.

1 *A Nation Prepared: Teachers for the 21st Century*. Washington, D.C.: Carnegie Forum on Education and the Economy, ©1986, p. 76. This report was prepared by the Carnegie Forum on Education and the Economy's Task Force on Teaching as a Profession. The Carnegie Forum is a program of the Carnegie Corporation of New York.

2 *Excellence in Professional Education*. Long Beach, Calif.: Office of the Chancellor, The California State University, (1983), p. 111.

TASK FORCE RECOMMENDATIONS

❶ **The Superintendent of Public Instruction, the State Board of Education, and the presidents of participating institutions of higher education and their respective boards should request the Legislature, Governor, and private foundations to collaborate in planning, funding, and implementing a partnership of 100 state-of-the-art middle grade schools and selected schools of education. The mission of this partnership should be to serve as a catalyst for the renewal and reform of middle grade education throughout California.**

❷ **Superintendents and local school boards should participate in the identification of participating middle grade schools through the processes of application and nomination; middle grade schools and schools of education ultimately selected for the partnership should be provided with appropriate administrative, logistical, and fiscal support.**

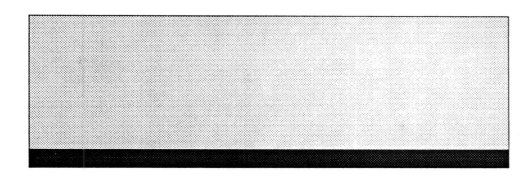

APPENDIX

Characteristics of Middle Grade Students [1]

A. Intellectual Development

Middle Grade Students:

1   Display a wide range of individual intellectual development as their minds experience transition from the concrete-manipulatory stage to the capacity for abstract thought. This transition ultimately makes possible:

- Propositional thought
- Consideration of ideas contrary to fact
- Reasoning with hypotheses involving two or more variables
- Appreciation for the elegance of mathematical logic expressed in symbols
- Insight into the nuances of poetic metaphor and musical notation
- Analysis of the power of a political ideology
- Ability to project thought into the future, to anticipate, and to formulate goals
- Insight into the sources of previously unquestioned attitudes, behaviors, and values
- Interpretation of larger concepts and generalizations of traditional wisdom expressed through sayings, axioms, and aphorisms

2   Are intensely curious;

3   Prefer active over passive learning experiences; favor interaction with peers during learning activities;

4   Exhibit a strong willingness to learn things they consider to be useful; enjoy using skills to solve real life problems;

5   Are egocentric; argue to convince others; exhibit independent, critical thought;

6   Consider academic goals as a secondary level of priority; personal-social concerns dominate thoughts and activities;

7   Experience the phenomenon of metacognition—the ability to know what one knows and does not know;

8   Are intellectually at-risk; face decisions that have the potential to affect major academic values with lifelong consequences.

---

1 Distilled from the writings of Bondi, Fenwick, Lipsitz, Mergendoller, Tye. (See Bibliography.)

B. Physical Development

Middle Grade Students:

1   Experience accelerated physical development marked by increases in weight, height, heart size, lung capacity, and muscular strength;

2   Mature at varying rates of speed. Girls tend to be taller than boys for the first two years of early adolescence and are ordinarily more physically developed than boys;

3   Experience bone growth faster than muscle development; uneven muscle/bone development results in lack of coordination and awkwardness; bones may lack protection of covering muscles and supporting tendons;

4   Reflect a wide range of individual differences which begin to appear in prepubertal and pubertal stages of development. Boys tend to lag behind girls. There are marked individual differences in physical development for boys and girls. The greatest variability in physiological development and size occurs at about age thirteen;

5   Experience biological development five years sooner than adolescents of the last century; the average age of menarche has dropped from seventeen to twelve years of age;

6   Face responsibility for sexual behavior before full emotional and social maturity has occurred;

7   Show changes in body contour including temporarily large noses, protruding ears, long arms; have posture problems;

8   Are often disturbed by body changes:

   •   Girls are anxious about physical changes that accompany sexual maturation;
   •   Boys are anxious about receding chins, cowlicks, dimples, and changes in their voices;

9   Experience fluctuations in basal metabolism which can cause extreme restlessness at times and equally extreme listlessness at other moments;

10 Have ravenous appetites and peculiar tastes; may overtax digestive system with large quantities of improper foods;

11 Lack physical health; have poor levels of endurance, strength, and flexibility; as a group are fatter and unhealthier;

12 Are physically at-risk; major causes of death are homicide, suicide, accident, and leukemia.

C. Psychological Development

Middle Grade Students:

1   Are often erratic and inconsistent in their behavior; anxiety and fear are contrasted with periods of bravado; feelings shift between superiority and inferiority;

2   Have chemical and hormonal imbalances which often trigger emotions that are frightening and poorly understood; may regress to more childish behavior patterns at this point;

3   Are easily offended and are sensitive to criticism of personal shortcomings;

4   Tend to exaggerate simple occurrences and believe that personal problems, experiences, and feelings are unique to themselves;

5   Are moody, restless; often feel self-conscious and alienated; lack self-esteem; are introspective;

6   Are searching for adult identity and acceptance even in the midst of intense peer group relationships;

7   Are vulnerable to naive opinions, one-sided arguments;

8   Are searching to form a conscious sense of individual uniqueness— "Who am I?";

9   Have emerging sense of humor based on increased intellectual ability to see abstract relationships; appreciate the "double entendre";

10 Are basically optimistic, hopeful;

11 Are psychologically at-risk; at no other point in human development is an individual likely to encounter so much diversity in relation to oneself and others.

D. Social Development

Middle Grade Students:

1   Experience often traumatic conflicts due to conflicting loyalties to peer groups and family;

2   Refer to peers as sources for standards and models of behavior; media heroes and heroines are also singularly important in shaping both behavior and fashion;

3   May be rebellious towards parents but still strongly dependent on parental values; want to make own choices, but the authority of the family is a critical factor in ultimate decisions;

4   Are impacted by high level of mobility in society; may become anxious and disoriented when peer group ties are broken because of family relocation to other communities;

5   Are often confused and frightened by new school settings which are large and impersonal;

6   Act out unusual or drastic behavior at times; may be aggressive, daring, boisterous, argumentative;

7   Are fiercely loyal to peer group values; sometimes cruel or insensitive to those outside the peer group;

8   Want to know and feel that significant adults, including parents and teachers, love and accept them; need frequent affirmation;

9   Sense negative impact of adolescent behaviors on parents and teachers; realize thin edge between tolerance and rejection; feelings of adult rejection drive the adolescent into the relatively secure social environment of the peer group;

10 Strive to define sex role characteristics; search to establish positive social relationships with members of the same and opposite sex;

11 Experience low risk-trust relationships with adults who show lack of sensitivity to adolescent characteristics and needs;

12 Challenge authority figures; test limits of acceptable behavior;

13 Are socially at-risk; adult values are largely shaped conceptually during adolescence; negative interactions with peers, parents, and teachers may compromise ideals and commitments.

E. Moral and Ethical Development

Middle Grade Students:

1   Are essentially idealistic; have a strong sense of fairness in human relationships;

2   Experience thoughts and feelings of awe and wonder related to their expanding intellectual and emotional awareness;

3   Ask large, unanswerable questions about the meaning of life; do not expect absolute answers but are turned off by trivial adult responses;

4   Are reflective, analytical, and introspective about their thoughts and feelings;

5   Confront hard moral and ethical questions for which they are unprepared to cope;

6   Are at-risk in the development of moral and ethical choices and behaviors; primary dependency on the influences of home and church for moral and ethical development seriously compromises adolescents for whom these resources are absent; adolescents want to explore the moral and ethical issues which are confronted in the curriculum, in the media, and in the daily interactions they experience in their families and peer groups.

Accountability Matrix

The following pages provide an accountability matrix for the recommendations found in the Report of the Middle Grade Task Force.   The horizontal axes indicate the levels of responsibility (Legislature, superintendents, etc.). The vertical axes indicate the categories of recommendations, including the page numbers where the complete text of each recommendation may be found.   The squares in the matrix show the numerical reference for each recommendation and a coded reference to the projected magnitude of the effort required for its implementation. The larger the number of ✍ signs, the greater the magnitude in terms of projected effort.

	Legislature; Governor		State Superintendent State Board of Education		State State Department of Education		Local/County District School Boards		Superintendents and Central Office Administrators	
Part One: Curriculum and Instruction										
1. Core Curriculum Pages 4-7							1.1a 1.1b 1.1c-f	✍✍ ✍✍✍ ✍✍		
2. Knowledge Pages 11-12							2.1.a(1-4) 2.1.b	✍ ✍	2.3	✍✍
3. Thinking and Communication Pages 18-19	3.3	✍✍					3.1a 3.1b	✍✍ ✍✍	3.2	✍✍
4. Character Development Pages 22-23										
5. Learning to Learn Pages 32-34					5.2 5.3 5.6	✍✍ ✍✍✍ ✍✍	5.1a 5.1b 5.1c 5.5 5.8 5.9 5.10 5.11	✍✍ ✍✍ ✍✍✍ ✍✍✍ ✍ ✍✍✍ ✍ ✍✍✍		
6. Instructional Practice Pages 43-46							6.1.a 6.1.b 6.1.c 6.1.d 6.1.e	✍ ✍ ✍ ✍ ✍✍✍		
Part Two: Student Potential										
7. Academic Counseling Pages 51-54					7.2	✍✍				
8. Equal Access Pages 57-58							8.1	✍	8.2a-g	✍✍✍
9. Student Diversity and Underrepresented Minorities Pages 62-64	9.5	✍✍✍✍			9.2	✍✍✍	9.1a-c	✍✍✍		
10. At-Risk Students Pages 69-70					10.4	✍✍✍	10.1a-c 10.3	✍ ✍✍✍	10.2 10.4	✍✍✍ ✍✍
11. Physical and Emotional Development Pages 75-77	11.1 11.3a-d 11.6	✍✍✍ ✍✍✍ ✍✍✍	11.1 11.3a-d	✍✍✍✍ ✍✍✍			11.2a-e 11.7 11.9	✍✍✍ ✍ ✍✍	11.4 11.8	✍✍ ✍

Principals		Teachers		Counselors		Colleges and Universities		Commission on Teacher Credentialing		
										1. Core Curriculum Pages 4-7
2.2 ☞☞ 2.3 ☞☞		2.2 ☞☞								2. Knowledge Pages 11-12
		3.2 ☞								3. Thinking and Communication Pages 18-19
4.2 ☞ 4.3 ☞		4.1a ☞☞☞ 4.1b ☞ 4.1c ☞☞☞ 4.2 ☞ 4.3 ☞		4.1a ☞☞☞ 4.1b ☞ 4.1c ☞☞☞ 4.2 ☞ 4.3 ☞						4. Character Development Pages 22-23
5.10 ☞		5.4 ☞☞ 5.7 ☞ 5.10 ☞								5. Learning to Learn Pages 32-34
6.2a ☞ 6.2b ☞☞☞ 6.3a ☞ 6.3b ☞ 6.3c ☞ 6.3d ☞☞☞		6.2a ☞ 6.2b ☞☞☞ 6.3a ☞ 6.3b ☞ 6.3c ☞ 6.3d ☞☞☞		6.2a ☞ 6.2b ☞☞☞ 6.3a ☞ 6.3b ☞ 6.3c ☞ 6.3d ☞☞☞						6. Instructional Practice Pages 43-46
7.1a-c ☞☞ 7.3a-g ☞☞☞ 7.4 ☞ 7.5a-h ☞☞☞		7.1a-c ☞☞ 7.3a-g ☞☞☞ 7.4 ☞ 7.5a-h ☞☞☞		7.1a-c ☞☞ 7.3a-g ☞☞☞ 7.4 ☞						7. Academic Counseling Pages 51-54
										8. Equal Access Pages 57-58
						9.3 ☞☞ 9.4 ☞☞☞				9. Student Diversity and Underrepresented Minorities Pages 62-64
10.2 ☞☞☞ 10.5 ☞☞ 10.6 ☞		10.6 ☞		10.6 ☞						10. At-Risk Students Pages 69-70
11.5 ☞☞ 11.8 ☞		11.5 ☞☞ 11.8 ☞		11.8 ☞						11. Physical and Emotional Development Pages 75-77

	Legislature; Governor		State Superintendent State Board of Education		State State Departmet of Education		Local/County District School Boards		Superintendents and Central Office Administrators	

Part Three: Organization and Structure

	Legislature; Governor		State Superintendent State Board of Education		State State Departmet of Education		Local/County District School Boards		Superintendents and Central Office Administrators	
12. School Culture Page 84					12.2	☞☞☞	12.2	☞☞☞	12.1a-f	☞☞
13. Extracurricular and Intramural Activities Page 86							13.1	☞		
14. Student Accountability Pages 89-90										
15. Transition Pages 96-97							15.1	☞	15.2a-c	☞☞☞
16. Structure Pages 102-105	16.2 16.3a-c 16.4a-f	☞☞☞☞ ☞☞☞☞ ☞☞☞☞	16.2 16.3a-c 16.4a-f	☞☞☞☞ ☞☞☞☞ ☞☞☞☞	16.6	☞☞	16.5a-c 16.7	☞☞☞ ☞☞	16.1a-b 16.8a-g	☞ ☞☞☞
17. Scheduling/ Philosophy Pages 110-111	17.5	☞☞☞			17.3 17.4	☞☞☞ ☞☞				
18. Assessment Pages 115-116					18.1 18.2	☞☞☞ ☞☞☞	18.3 18.4a-g 18.5	☞☞ ☞☞ ☞	18.5	☞

Part Four: Teaching and Administration

	Legislature; Governor		State Superintendent State Board of Education		State State Departmet of Education		Local/County District School Boards		Superintendents and Central Office Administrators	
19. Professional Preparation Pages 123-124							19.2 19.7	☞☞ ☞☞☞	19.3	☞☞☞
20. Staff Development Pages 130-132	20.1a-c	☞☞☞☞							20.2a-d 20.3a-d 20.4a-d	☞☞☞ ☞☞☞ ☞☞

Part Five: Leadership and Partnership

	Legislature; Governor		State Superintendent State Board of Education		State State Departmet of Education		Local/County District School Boards		Superintendents and Central Office Administrators	
21. Parents, Communities, and School Boards Pages 138-139			21.1 21.2 21.3	☞☞☞ ☞☞☞ ☞☞	21.7	☞☞	21.4 21.6	☞ ☞☞☞	21.5	☞☞☞
22. State-of-the-Art Middle Grade Schools Page 142	22.1	☞☞☞☞	22.1	☞☞☞☞			22.2	☞☞	22.2	☞☞

Principals		Teachers		Counselors		Colleges and Universities		Commission on Teacher Credentialing		153
12.1a-f	☞☞	12.1a-f	☞☞	12.1a-f	☞☞					12. School Culture Page 84
13.2 13.3 13.4	☞☞ ☞ ☞	13.4 13.5 13.6	☞ ☞ ☞	13.4	☞					13. Extracurricular and Intramural Activities Page 86
14.1a-d 14.2a-f	☞ ☞	14.1a-d 14.2a-f	☞ ☞	14.1a-d 14.2a-f	☞ ☞					14. Student Accountability Pages 89-90
15.3a-e	☞☞	15.3a-e	☞☞	15.3a-e	☞☞					15. Transition Pages 96-97
16.1a-b 16.8a-g	☞ ☞☞☞									16. Structure Pages 102-105
17.1a-g 17.2	☞☞☞ ☞	17.1a-g 17.2	☞☞☞ ☞	17.1a-g 17.2	☞☞☞ ☞					17. Scheduling/ Philosophy Pages 110-111
18.5	☞	18.5	☞	18.5	☞					18. Assessment Pages 115-116
						19.3 19.4 19.5	☞☞☞ ☞☞ ☞☞☞	19.1a-b 19.3 19.6	☞☞☞ ☞☞☞ ☞	19. Professional Preparation Pages 123-124
20.4a-d	☞☞									20. Staff Development Pages 130-132
										21. Parents, Communities, and School boards Pages 138-139
										22. State-of-the-Art Middle Grade Schools Page 142

Selected Bibliography: Middle Grade Education

Books

Adolescent Socialization in Cross-Cultural Perspective. Edited by Irving Tallman, and Ramon Marotz-Braden. Orlando, Fla.: Academic Press, 1983.

An Agenda for Excellence at the Middle Level. Reston, Va.: National Association of Secondary School Principals, 1985.

Blos, Peter. *The Adolescent Passage: Developmental Issues.* New York: International Universities Press, 1979.

Boyer, Ernest. *High School: A Report on Secondary Education in America.* The Carnegie Foundation for the Advancement of Teaching and Ernest L. Boyer. New York: Harper and Row, 1983.

Chilman, Catherine S. *Adolescent Sexuality in a Changing American Society: Social and Psychological Perspectives for the Human Service Professions (Second edition).* New York: John Wiley and Sons, Inc., 1983.

Developing Minds: A Resource Book for Teaching Thinking. Edited by Arthur L. Costa. Alexandria, Va.: Association for Supervision and Curriculum Development, 1985.

Excellence in Professional Education: A Report of the Advisory Committee to Study Programs in Education in The California State University. Long Beach, Calif.: Office of the Chancellor, The California State University, 1983.

Farrar, Eleanor, and Arthur G. Powell. *The Shopping Mall High School: Winners and Losers in the Educational Marketplace.* Boston, Mass.: Houghton Mifflin Co., 1985.

Fenwick, James J. *The Middle School Years.* San Diego, Calif.: Fenwick Associates, 1986.

Futures: Making High School Count. Glendale, Calif.: California Round Table on Educational Opportunity, 1983.

George, Paul S. *The Theory Z School: Beyond Effectiveness.* The National Middle School Association, 1983.

Goodlad, John I. *A Place Called School.* New York: McGraw-Hill Book Company, 1984.

Handbook of Adolescents and Family Therapy. Edited by Stuart L. Korman and Marsha Pravder. New York: Gardner Press, 1985.

Hispanics and Higher Education: Final Report of the Commission on Hispanic Underrepresentation. Long Beach, Calif.: The California State University, 1985.

Honig, Bill. *Last Chance for Our Children: How You Can Help Save Our Schools.* Reading, Mass.: Addison-Wesley Publishing Company, Inc., 1986.

Kirst, Michael. *Who Controls Our Schools?* New York: W.H. Freeman and Co., 1985.

Lipsitz, Joan. *Successful Schools for Young Adolescents.* New Brunswick, N.J.: Transaction Books, 1984.

Lueptow, Lloyd B. *Adolescent Sex Roles and Social Change.* New York: Columbia University Press, 1984.

Mathematics Framework for California Public Schools—Kindergarten Through Grade Twelve. Sacramento: California State Department of Education, 1985.

Mergendoller, John , and Virginia Marchman. *Friends and Associates; Educators Handbook: Research into Practice.* White Plains, N.Y.: Longman, Inc., 1987.

A Nation Prepared: Teachers for the 21st Century. Washington, D.C.: Carnegie Forum on Education and the Economy, 1986.

Roueche, John, and George Baker, III, *Profiling Excellence in American Schools.* Arlington, Vir.: American Association of School Administrators, 1986.

Schwendinger, Herman, and Julia Siegel Schwendinger. *Adolescent Subcultures and Delinquincy.* (Research edition). New York: Praeger Publications, 1985.

Secondary School Program Quality Criteria. Prepared by the Office of School Improvement, California State Department of Education. Sacramento: California State Department of Education, 1985.

Seltzer, Vivian Center. *Adolescent Social Development: Dynamic Functional Interaction.* Lexington, Mass.: Lexington Books, 1982.

Skager, Rodney, Dennis Fisher, and Ebrahim Maddahiam. *A Statewide Survey of Drug and Alcohol Use Among California Students in Grades 7, 9, and 11.* Sacramento: Office of the Attorney General, May, 1986.

Symposium on Pediatric and Adolescent Sports Medicine. Edited by James M. Betts and Martin Eichelberger. Philadelphia: Saunders, 1982.

Tye, Kenneth. *The Junior High: A School in Search of a Mission.* Lanham, Md.: University Press of America, 1985.

What Works: Research About Teaching and Learning. Prepared under the direction of William J. Bennett. Washington, D.C.: United States Department of Education, 1986.

Who Will Teach Our Children?—A Strategy for Improving California's Schools (The Commons Report). Sacramento: California Commission on the Teaching Profession, 1985.

Wiles, Jon, and Joseph Bondi, Jr. *The Essential Middle School.* Columbus, Ohio: Charles E. Merrill Publishing Co., 1981.

Wiles, Jon, and Joseph Bondi, Jr. *Making Middle Schools Work.* Alexandria, Va.: Association for Supervision and Curriculum Development, 1987.

Articles

(The majority of these citations are available through ERIC.)

Alexander, William M., and C. Kenneth McEwin. "Middle Level Schools—Their Status and Their Promise," *NASSP Bulletin*, Vol. 70 (January, 1986), 90--95.

Alexander, William M., and C. Kenneth McEwin. "Training the Middle Level Educator— Where Does the Solution Lie?" *NASSP Bulletin*, Vol. 68 (September, 1984), 6--11.

Arth, Alfred A., and others. "Introducing Competition to the Middle Level Classroom: Providing for Success," *NASSP Bulletin*, Vol. 68 (September, 1984), 63--68.

Beane, James A. "Self-Concept and Esteem in the Middle Level School," *NASSP Bulletin*, Vol. 67 (May, 1983), 63--71.

Beane, James A. "The Self-Enhancing Middle-Grade School," *School Counselor*, Vol. 33 (January, 1986), 189--95.

Bergmann, Sherrel, and Jeanne Baxter. "Building a Guidance Program and Advisory Concept for Early Adolescents," *NASSP Bulletin*, Vol. 67 (May, 1983), 49--55.

Bibby, Elaine. "A Small School in a Big School District," *Small School Forum*, Vol. 5 (Winter, 1983-84), 4--6.

Bloomer, Joan M. "Middle Level: Conquering the New Frontier," *NASSP Bulletin*, Vol. 70 (February, 1986), 95--96.

Blumenfeld, P., J. Mergendoller, and D. Swarthout, "Tasks as Heuristic," *Journal of Curriculum Studies*, Vol. 19 (Spring, 1987), pp. 134--47.

Bough, Max. "Middle School Curriculum—Does It Meet the Needs of the Transescent Child?" *Contemporary Education*, Vol. 54 (Summer, 1983), 272--74.

Bowers, Janice L., and Karen S. Farr. "Study Skills—A Must at the Middle School Level," *NASSP Bulletin*, Vol. 68 (January, 1984), 121--23.

Bowman, Robert P. "Peer Facilitator Programs for Middle Graders: Students Helping Each Other Grow Up," *School Counselor*, Vol. 33 (January, 1986), 221--29.

Brimm, Paul, and Charles E. Moore. "A Teacher-Advisor Plan in the Junior High/Middle School," *North Central Association Quarterly*, Vol. 59 (Winter, 1985), 352--60.

Carter, Betty, and Karen Harris. "What Junior High Students Like in Books," *Journal of Reading*, Vol. 26 (October, 1982), 42--46.

Clark, Sally N., and Donald C. Clark. "Creating a Responsive Middle Level School Through Systematic Long-Range Planning," *NASSP Bulletin*, Vol. 68 (September, 1984), 42--51.

Cook, Ronald E. "Five Steps to a Better School Climate," *NASSP Bulletin*, Vol. 67 (May, 1983), 121--22.

Damico, Sandra Bowman, and Christopher Sparks, "Cross-Group Contact Opportunities: Impact on Interpersonal Relationships in Desegregated Middle Schools," *Sociology of Education*, Vol. 59 (April, 1986), 113--23.

Damico, Sandra Bowman; and others. "The Impact of School Organization on Interracial Contact Among Students," *Journal of Educational Equity and Leadership*, Vol. 2 (Summer, 1982), 238--52.

Delaney, John D. "Developing a Middle School Homeroom Guidance Program,"
NASSP Bulletin, Vol. 70 (February, 1986), 96--98.

Deller, Don K. "Achieving Excellence in Today's Middle School—What Is Required?"
NASSP Bulletin, Vol. 68 (September, 1984), 19--24.

Dembo, Richard, and others. "Supports for and Consequences of Early Drug Involvement
Among Inner City Junior High School Youths Living in Three Neighborhood
Settings," *Journal of Drug Education*, Vol. 12 (1982), 191--210.

Dorman, Gale. "Making Schools Work for Young Adolescents," *Educational Horizons*,
Vol. 61 (Summer, 1983), 173--182.

Eichhorn, Donald H. "Focus on the Learner Leads to a Clearer Middle Level Picture,"
NASSP Bulletin, Vol. 67 (May, 1983), 45--48.

Elkind, David. "Stress and the Middle Grader," *School Counselor*, Vol. 33 (January,
1986), 196--206.

Estrada, Antonio, and others. "Alcohol Use Among Hispanic Adolescents: A Preliminary
Report," *Hispanic Journal of Behavioral Sciences*, Vol. 4 (September, 1982), 339--51.

Fibkins, William L. " What Makes a Middle School Excellent?" *Principal*, Vol. 64
(March, 1985), 50--51.

Fillenberg, Carol K. "Tips on Planning the Middle Level School." *NASSP Bulletin*,
Vol. 68 (September, 1984), 34--38.

Ford, Denyce S. "Factors Related to the Anticipated Use of Drugs by Urban Junior High
School Students," *Journal of Drug Education*, Vol. 13 (1983), 187--96.

Garawski, Robert A. "Middle School 'Walking Advisement': A Model for Successful
Implementation," *Clearing House*, Vol. 56 (September, 1982), 5--7.

George, Paul S. "The Counselor and Modern Middle-Level Schools: New Roles in New
Schools," *School Counselor*, Vol. 33 (January, 1986), 178--88.

George, Paul S. "A Response to Yoder: But We Do Need Good Middle Level Schools,"
Educational Leadership, Vol. 40 (November, 1982), 50--51.

George, Paul S., and Lynn L. Oldaker. "A National Survey of Middle School
Effectiveness," *Educational Leadership*, Vol. 43 (December, 1985--January, 1986),
79--85.

Greenleaf, Warren T. "Profile of the Middle School Principal," *Principal*, Vol. 62
(March, 1983), 30--33.

Grumaer, Jim. "Working in Groups with Middle Grades," *School Counselor*, Vol. 33
(January, 1986), 230--38.

Henson, Kenneth T. "Middle Schools: Paradoxes and Promises," *Clearing House*,
Vol. 59 (April, 1986), 345--47.

Hertsgaard, Doris, and Harriet Light. "Junior High Girls' Attitudes Toward the Rights
and Roles of Women," *Adolescence*, Vol. 19 (Winter, 1984), 847--53.

Hertzog, C. Jay. "The Middle School Today—Are Programs Up-to-Date?" *NASSP
Bulletin*, Vol. 68 (May, 1984), 108--10.

Hirsch, E.D., Jr. "Cultural Literacy," *The American Scholar*, Vol. 52 (Spring, 1983),
159--69.

Hollingsworth, Patricia L. "Coppola Brings the Outsiders In," *Phi Delta Kappan*, Vol. 64 (October, 1982), 130--31.

Jenkins, Joseph, and Linda Jenkins. "Peer Tutoring in Elementary and Secondary Programs," *Focus on Exceptional Children*, Vol. 17 (February, 1985), pp. 1--12.

Kienapfel, Bruce. "Supervision of Curriculum at the Middle Level," *NASSP Bulletin*, Vol. 68 (September, 1984), 52--57.

Kierstead, Janet. "Direct Instruction and Experiential Approaches: Are They Really Mutually Exclusive?" *Educational Leadership*, Vol. 42 (May, 1985), pp. 25--30.

Kierstead, Janet. "How Teachers Manage Individual and Small-Group Work in Active Classrooms," *Educational Leadership*, Vol. 44 (October, 1986), pp. 22--25.

Klingele, William E. "Middle Level Education: Do We Need It?" *Clearing House*, Vol. 58 (April, 1985), 334--36.

Kripp, Judy-Arin, and Robert A. Parker. "Preparing Your Child for Junior High," *PTA Today*, Vol. 10 (May, 1985), 8--9.

Kurdek, Lawrence A., and Donna Krile. "A Developmental Analysis of the Relation Between Peer Acceptance and Both Interpersonal Understanding and Perceived Social Self-Competence," *Child Development*, Vol. 53 (December,1982), 1485--91.

La Torre, Ronald A., and others. "Gender-Role Adoption and Sex as Academic and Psychological Risk Factors," *Sex Roles: A Journal of Research*, Vol. 9 (November, 1983), 127--36.

Lerner, Bao-Ting, and Carol G. Crawford, "Great Expectations—Challenging the Interests of the Gifted and Talented Junior High Student," *Mathematics Teacher*, Vol. 77 (January, 1984), 21--26.

Levine, Daniel U., and others. " Characteristics of Effective Inner-City Intermediate Schools," *Phi Delta Kappan*, Vol. 65 (June, 1984), 707--11.

Lipsitz, Joan, and others. "Grade Organization in the Middle Grades: Is There a 'Best' Solution?" *Spectrum*, Vol. 3 (Winter, 1985), 18--22.

Lounsbury, John H. "Developing Effective Middle Level Schools—It's the Principal of the Thing," *NASSP Bulletin*, Vol. 67 (May, 1983), 8--13.

Maskowitz, Joel M., and others. " The Effects of Drug Education at Follow-Up," *Journal of Alcohol and Drug Education*, Vol. 30 (Fall, 1984), 45--49.

Maultsby, Maxie C., Jr. "Teaching Rational Self-Counseling to Middle Graders," *School Counselor*, Vol. 33 (January, 1986), 207--19.

McEwin, C. Kenneth. "Middle Level Teacher Education and Certification," *NASSP Bulletin*, Vol. 67 (May, 1983), 78--82.

McEwin, C. Kenneth. "Schools for Early Adolescents," *Theory into Practice*, Vol. 22 (Spring, 1983), 119--24.

Merenbloom, Elliot Y. "Staff Development: The Key to Effective Middle Level Schools," *NASSP Bulletin*, Vol. 68 (September, 1984), 24--33.

Mitchum, Nancy Taylor. "Introducing TIP: The Total Involvement Program for Peer Facilitators," *School Counselor*, Vol. 31 (November, 1983), 146--49.

Oliver, Teddy J., and Robert D. Clements. "Middle School Expressions," *School Arts*, Vol. 83 (September, 1983), 24--27.

Patton, James E., and others. "Where Do Children Study? " *Journal of Educational Research*, Vol. 76 (May-June, 1983), 280--86.

Preston, Frederick B. "A Behavior Management Plan for Middle Level Students," *NASSP Bulletin*, Vol. 68 (September, 1984), 39--41.

Randhawa, Bikkar S. "Verbal Interaction of Students and Their Teachers in Junior High Classroom," *American Educational Research Journal*, Vol. 20 (Winter, 1983), 671--86.

Resnick, Daniel P., and Lauran B. Resnick. "Standards, Curriculum, and Performance: A Historical and Comparative Perspective," *Educational Researcher*, Vol. 14 (April, 1985), 5--20.

St. Clair, Robert. " In Search of Excellence at the Middle Level," *NASSP Bulletin*, Vol. 68 (September, 1984), 1--5.

Schmidt, Donald J., and J. Thomas Kane. "Solving an Identity Crisis," *Principal*, Vol. 63 (January, 1984), 32--35.

"Special Focus on Peer Helpers," Edited by Robert P. Bowman. *Elementary School Guidance and Counseling*, Vol. 18 (December, 1983), 111--46.

Steele, Chery A. "The Truths of Transescence," *Principal*, Vol. 65 (November, 1985), 50--52.

Thomason, Julia, and Billy Williams. "Middle Schools Are for Me," *Educational Leadership*, Vol. 40 (November, 1982), 54--58.

Thornberg, Hershel D. "The Counselor's Impact on Middle-Grade Students," *School Counselor*, Vol. 33 (January, 1986), 170--77.

Thornberg, Hershel D. "Middle-Level Education: A Researcher Speaks," *Action in Teacher Education*, Vol. 6 (Fall, 1984), 65--72.

Valentine, Jerry W. "A National Study of Schools in the Middle—Perspectives on Five Issues," *NASSP Bulletin*, Vol. 68 (September, 1984), 12--18.

Walker, Lawrence J., and others. "The Hierarchical Nature of Stages of Moral Development," *Developmental Psychology*, Vol. 20 (September, 1984), 960--66.

Whitfield, Edie L., and others. "Middle School Staff Development," *Clearing House*, Vol. 56 (January, 1983), 230--31.

Williams, James J., and Norris M. Haynes. "Black Junior High School Students' Perception of the Role and Effectiveness of Counselors," *Journal of Non-White Concerns in Personnel and Guidance*, Vol. 11 (July, 1983), 152--56.

Yoder, Walter H., Jr. "Middle School vs. Junior High Misses the Point," *Educational Leadership*, Vol. 40 (November, 1982), 50.

Publications Available from the Department of Education

This publication is one of over 600 that are available from the California Department of Education. Some of the more recent publications or those most widely used are the following:

Item no.	Title (Date of publication)	Price
1317	Adult Education Handbook for California (1997 Edition)	$15.00
1372	Arts Work: A Call for Arts Education for All California Students (1997)	11.25
1379	Assessing and Fostering the Development of a First and a Second Language in Early Childhood—Training Manual (1998)	19.00
1377	Assessing the Development of a First and a Second Language: Resource Guide (1998)	10.75
1356	Best Practices for Designing and Delivering Effective Programs for Individuals with Autistic Spectrum Disorders (1997)	10.00
1376	California School Accounting Manual, 1997 Edition (updates item 1025) (1997)	10.50 *
1396	California Special Education Programs: A Composite of Laws (1998)	no charge
0488	Caught in the Middle: Educational Reform for Young Adolescents in California Public Schools (1987)	9.25
1297	Challenge Standards for Student Success: Language Arts (1997)	10.00
1298	Challenge Standards for Student Success: Mathematics (1997)	15.75
1290	Challenge Toolkit: Family-School Compact (1997)	9.95
1300	Challenge Toolkit: Outline for Assessment and Accountability Plans (1997)	12.75
1299	Challenge Toolkit: Safe and Healthy Schools (1997)	14.25
1294	Challenge Toolkit: School Facilities (1997)	11.75
1295	Challenge Toolkit: Site-Based Decision Making (1997)	14.25
1291	Challenge Toolkit: Service Learning (1997)	8.75
1292	Challenge Toolkit: Student Activities (1997)	9.25
1296	Challenge Toolkit: Student Learning Plans (1997)	7.75
1375	Children Teaching Children (CD-ROM) (1997)	12.00
1359	A Child's Place in the Environment, Unit 1: Respecting Living Things, Student Pages in Spanish (1997)	9.75
1360	A Child's Place in the Environment, Unit 2: Protecting Soil, Student Pages in Spanish (1997)	9.75
1361	A Child's Place in the Environment, Unit 3: Preserving and Restoring Ecosystems, Student Pages in Spanish (1998)	12.00
1281	Connect, Compute, and Compete: The Report of the California Education Technology Task Force (1996)	5.75
1285	Continuity for Young Children (1997)	7.50
1034	Course Models for the History–Social Science Framework, Grade Six—World History and Geography: Ancient Civilizations (1993)	12.00
1132	Course Models for the History–Social Science Framework, Grade Seven—World History and Geography: Medieval and Early Modern Times (1994)	15.25
1247	Course Models for the History–Social Science Framework, Grade Ten—World History, Culture, and Geography: The Modern World (1995)	18.50
1352	Educational Specifications: Linking Design of School Facilities to Educational Program (1997)	18.50
1215	English-as-a-Second-Language Handbook for Adult Education Instructors, 1995 Edition (1995)	10.25
0041	English–Language Arts Framework for California Public Schools (1987)	7.25
1244	Every Child a Reader: The Report of the California Reading Task Force (1995)	5.25
1367	Family Connections: Helping Caregivers Develop Nutrition Partnerships with Parents (1997)	9.00
1388	First Look: Vision Evaluation and Assessment for Infants, Toddlers, and Preschoolers, Birth Through Five Years of Age (1998)	10.00
0804	Foreign Language Framework for California Public Schools (1989)	7.25
1355	The Form of Reform: School Facility Design Implications for California Educational Reform (1997)	18.50
1378	Fostering the Development of a First and a Second Language: Resource Guide (1998)	10.75
1365	Fresh Fruit and Vegetable Photo Cards (1997)	30.00
1382	Getting Results, Part I: California Action Guide to Creating Safe and Drug-Free Schools and Communities (1998)	15.25
1268	Guidelines for Occupational Therapy and Physical Therapy in California Public Schools (1996)	12.50
1064	Health Framework for California Public Schools, Kindergarten Through Grade Twelve (1994)	10.00
1322	Helping Your Child with Homework (1997)	6.25
0737	Here They Come: Ready or Not—Report of the School Readiness Task Force (summary report) (1988)	5.00
1284	History–Social Science Framework for California Public Schools, 1997 Updated Edition (1997)	12.50
1245	Improving Mathematics Achievement for All California Students: The Report of the California Mathematics Task Force (1995)	5.25
1258	Industrial and Technology Education: Career Path Guide and Model Curriculum Standards (1996)	17.00
1269	Instructional Materials Approved for Legal Compliance, 1996 Edition	23.00
1147	It's Elementary! (Abridged Version) (1994)	Set of 10/6.00
1024	It's Elementary! Elementary Grades Task Force Report (1992)	9.00

*Contains Part II, the Standardized Account Code Structure, and supplements Part I.

Item no.	Title (Date of publication)	Price
1252	Just Kids: A Training Manual for Working with Children Prenatally Substance-Exposed (1996)	22.25
1227	Keeping Kids Healthy: Preventing and Managing Communicable Disease in Child Care (1995)	15.00
1266	Literature for the Visual and Performing Arts, Kindergarten Through Grade Twelve (1996)	10.25
1216	Martin Luther King, Jr., 1929–1968 (1995)	7.50
1033	Mathematics Framework for California Public Schools, 1992 Edition	8.00
1183	Meeting the Challenge: A History of Adult Education in California—From the Beginnings to the 1990s (1995)	13.50
1213	Model Program Standards for Adult Basic Education (1996)	11.50
1248	Model Program Standards for Adult Secondary Education (1996)	11.50
1384	Observing Preschoolers: Assessing First and Second Language Development (video) (1998)	12.00
1065	Physical Education Framework for California Public Schools, Kindergarten Through Grade Twelve (1994)	7.75
1222	Practical Ideas for Teaching Writing as a Process at the High School and College Levels (1997)	18.00
1221	Practical Ideas for Teaching Writing as a Process at the Elementary School and Middle School Levels (1996 Revised Edition)	18.00
1289	Program Guidelines for Students Who Are Visually Impaired (1997)	10.00
1256	Project EXCEPTIONAL: A Guide for Training and Recruiting Child Care Providers to Serve Young Children with Disabilities, Volume 1 (1996)	20.00
1257	Project EXCEPTIONAL: A Guide for Training and Recruiting Child Care Providers to Serve Young Children with Disabilities, Volume 2 (1996)	30.75
1344	Reading/Language Arts and English as a Second Language: Adoption Report (1997)	11.00
1399	Ready to Learn: Quality Preschools for California in the 21st Century (1998)	8.00
1171	Recommended Readings in Literature, Kindergarten Through Grade Eight, Revised Annotated Edition (1996)	10.00
1315	Reducing Exceptional Stress and Trauma: Curriculum and Intervention Guidelines (1997)	17.00
1316	Reducing Exceptional Stress and Trauma: Facilitator's Guide (1997)	18.00
1318	Room at the Table: Meeting Children's Special Needs at Mealtimes (video and guide) (1997)	17.00
1246	School Attendance Review Boards Handbook: Operations and Resources (1995)	7.00
1150	School-Age Care in California: Addressing the Needs of Children, Families, and Society (1996)	13.00
0870	Science Framework for California Public Schools (1990)	9.50
1387	School District Organization Handbook (1998)	24.50
1040	Second to None: A Vision of the New California High School (1992)	9.50
1407	Steering by Results: A High-Stakes Rewards and Interventions Program for California Schools and Students (1998)	8.00
1277	Strategies for Success: A Resource Manual for SHAPE (Shaping Health as Partners in Education) (1996)	15.00
1383	Talking with Preschoolers: Strategies for Promoting First and Second Language Development (video) (1998)	12.00
1255	Taking Charge: Disaster Preparedness Guide for Child Care and Development Centers (1996)	10.25
1276	Teaching Reading: A Balanced, Comprehensive Approach to Teaching Reading in Prekindergarten Through Grade Three (1996)	5.75
1260	Today's Special: A Fresh Approach to Meals for Preschoolers (video and guide) (1996)	17.00*
1342	Transportation Demand Management: Data Analysis, Instructor's Edition (1997)	14.00
1335	Transportation Demand Management: Investigations and Problem Analysis—A Science Resource Unit, Grades Eight–Twelve (1997)	11.00
1337	Transportation Demand Management: Transportation Choices, Instructor's Edition (1997)	11.00
1261	Visual and Performing Arts Framework for California Public Schools, Kindergarten Through Grade Twelve (1996)	15.00
1392	Work-Based Learning Guide (1998)	12.50
1390	Work Permit Handbook (1998)	13.00

*Also available in a Spanish edition of both video and guide (item no. 1262) at same price.

Orders should be directed to:

California Department of Education
Publications Division, Sales Office
P.O. Box 271
Sacramento, CA 95812-0271

Please include the item number and desired quantity for each title ordered. Shipping and handling charges are additional, and purchasers in California also add county sales tax.

Mail orders must be accompanied by a check, a purchase order, or a credit card number, including expiration date (VISA or MasterCard only). Purchase orders without checks are accepted from educational institutions, businesses, and governmental agencies. Telephone orders will be accepted toll-free (1-800-995-4099) for credit card purchases. *All sales are final.*

The *Educational Resources Catalog* contains illustrated, annotated listings of departmental publications, videos, and other instructional materials. Free copies of the *Catalog* may be obtained by writing to the address given above or by calling (916) 445-1260.

R98-024   (Fourteenth printing) 003-0026-98 300 11-98 3,500